HUMMINGBIRDS

HUMMINGBIRDS

A Wildlife Handbook

Kim Long

SCIENTIFIC ADVISOR
Bill Alther, zoologist

Johnson Books
BOULDER

Published in the United States by Johnson Books, a division of Johnson Publishing Company, 1880 South 57th Court, Boulder, Colorado 80301.

9 8 7 6 5 4 3 2 1

Cover design: Margaret Donharl
Cover illustration: Kim Long

All illustrations by the author unless otherwise indicated.

Library of Congress Cataloging-in-Publication Data
    Long, Kim
        Hummingbirds: a wildlife handbook / Kim Long.
            p. cm. — (Johnson nature series)
        Includes bibliographical references and index.
        ISBN 1-55566-188-2 (alk. paper)
            1. Hummingbirds. I. Title. II. Series
    QL696.A558L66 1997   96-49302
    598.7'64—dc21   CIP

Printed in the United States by
Johnson Printing
1880 South 57th Court
Boulder, Colorado 80301

♻ Printed on recycled paper with soy ink

CONTENTS

ACKNOWLEDGMENTS

Dr. Randall Lockwood, Humane Society of the U.S.
Guy Hodge, Humane Society of the U.S.
Gregory McNamee
Bill Alther, Denver Museum of Natural History
The Bloomsbury Review
Denver Public Library
Western History Collection, Denver Public Library
Norlin Library, University of Colorado
Auraria Library, Metropolitan State College
Stage House II Books, Boulder, Colorado
Sande Corbett and Paul Hardy,
   Ramsey Canyon Preserve, Hereford, Arizona
Wild Birds Unlimited
The urban waifs at The Cup, Tucson, Arizona

INTRODUCTION

Except for robins and pigeons, no birds in North America are so readily identified by so many people as are hummingbirds. These flitting creatures can be seen throughout Canada and the United States in the summer months and have a magnetic quality, attracting viewers both young and old, mesmerizing by their sight and sound. Harmless, beautiful, and often close-at-hand, hummingbirds represent nature at its most attractive to a growing population of lovers of wildlife. Unlike the more majestic aerial predators — hawks, eagles, and owls — hummingbirds may be readily found in urban settings, parks, and suburban backyards, making them an accessible symbol.

Unique to this hemisphere, the first European explorers brought back descriptions of these birds that made them sound like mythical, tiny jeweled creatures buzzing through the air and performing impossible feats of aerial acrobatics. The first exhibitions of mounted hummingbirds attracted the attentions and wonderment of royalty, that eventually resulted in their being hunted as a valuable fashion accessory. Luckily, decades of wanton killing that turned millions of hummingbirds into women's hats stopped before they became extinct, a fate unfortunately not shared by other birds with attractive plumage.

Today, hummingbirds thrive in most parts of this continent, but their reproduction is increasingly threatened by the reduction of native habitats. The relentless expansion of cities, the construction of new roads, dams, and parking lots, and the destruction of natural stands of flowering food sources are all negative forces that threaten the long-term health of these birds. The hummingbird has become a new visible symbol for the health of the environment — where they thrive, nature is still in balance.

THE TALE OF THE HUMMINGBIRD

"If God thus preserves some small birds and afterward resurrects them, and year by year one sees these marvels in this land, who would doubt of human bodies, which are buried corruptible, that God shall not resurrect them incorruptible by Jesus Christ, and that he will dress and adorn them with the four gifts, and sustain them with the tenderness of his divine fruition and vision, since he sustains these small birds with the dew and honey of flowers, and dresses them with such gracious feathers, that not even Solomon in his splendor was dressed as one of these."
— Toribio de Motolinía

In the western hemisphere, hummingbirds are a common sight and have figured prominently in the myths and legends of most native cultures. But unlike most other types of birds, no similar species exists outside of North and South America. In Europe and Asia, the concept of such a small bird, able to hover in mid-flight, was unknown until the first explorers brought back descriptions from their travels.

Among the pueblo tribes of the southwest, the hummingbird often appeared as a symbol. In the Acoma pueblo tradition, Hummingbird is a special messenger used by the Gods. Hopi pueblos share an origin myth describing how shamans use Hummingbird as a courier, sending gifts from humans to the Mother, known as Iyatiku, who lives in the lowest world. Generally, the pueblo religions attribute to the hummingbird the power of rain — the ability to create precipitation — a powerful force in an arid region. The Pimas go even further, believing these birds could also summon wind.

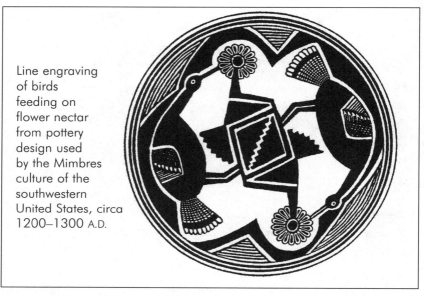

Line engraving of birds feeding on flower nectar from pottery design used by the Mimbres culture of the southwestern United States, circa 1200–1300 A.D.

A traditional myth of the Cherokee tells of a pretty woman who was wooed by the Hummingbird and the Crane. She preferred the Hummingbird because he was so handsome, but the Crane was very persistent, forcing her to challenge the two suitors to a race around the world, with the winner gaining her hand in marriage. Secretly, she expected the Hummingbird to win, as he flew so fast. But the Crane had his own secret: he could fly all night. So while the Hummingbird flew ahead during the day, he had to stop and sleep when night came. After seven days of racing, the Crane was the first to arrive back at the starting point. Disappointed, the maiden declared she could never have such an ugly thing for a husband, and decided to stay single. The Creek tribe has a similar myth, in which the Crane wins because it flies in a straight line, while the Hummingbird wastes time zipping back and forth following the path of a stream.

Hummingbirds also appear in other Indian myths as a similar

force, providing an element of speed to overcome obstacles or enemies. An ancient myth of the Fox tribe describes how ceremonial runners were blessed by a succession of spirits: the wind, a deer, and a hummingbird. These forces combined to make them excellent runners. In a Menomini myth, "The Race With the Witch," is another example of the hummingbird spirit. In this tale, the hero, Ball Carrier, is involved in a prolonged foot race with his sister-in-law, who was a witch. The winner is given the privilege of slaying the loser. During the race, Ball Carrier changes himself into different animals, including the Wolf, the Crow, the Pigeon, and several different hawks. But during each transformation, he eventually tires, allowing the witch to catch up and pass him. Finally, nearing home and running behind the witch, Ball Carrier changes himself into Na-na-tska, the Hummingbird, and shoots into the lead. Arriving first, he throws off his animal form and seizing his warclub, strikes the witch on the head when she arrives, killing her.

A Cochiti Indian myth is "Hummingbird Has Food," in which the people lose faith with the creator, "Our Mother." They ceased to believe that it was she who sent the rain. Angry, Our Mother hid the clouds and for four years there was no rain. The only creature who did not suffer during this period was Hummingbird, who had been told by Our Mother to expect the long, dry period, and had been given a secret, the directions to shipap (entrance to the underworld), where Hummingbird could find honey in the flowers. Seeing her remain strong and fat, the people asked Hummingbird many times where Our Mother had gone, but Hummingbird always answered that she did not know, following the instructions that Our Mother had given her. After a long spell of suffering, the people finally understood what had happened, that it really was Our Mother who brought them rain and provided the food they ate.

The Arawaks, an extinct tribe native to some Caribbean islands, believed that the hummingbird carried tobacco to their people for the first time. Because the birds were associated with tobacco, and

THOREAU'S HUMMINGBIRDS

May 17, 1856. Meanwhile I hear a loud hum and see a splendid male hummingbird coming zigzag in long tracks, like a bee, but far swifter, along the edge of the swamp, in hot haste. He turns aside to taste the honey of the Andromeda calyculata (already visited by bees) within a rod of me. This golden-green gem. Its burnished back looks as if covered with green scales dusted with gold. It hovers, as it were stationary in the air, with an intense humming before each little flower-bell of the humble Andromeda calyculata, and inserts its long tongue in each, turning toward me that splendid ruby on its breast, that glowing ruby. Even this is coal-black in some lights! There, along with me in the deep, wild swamp, above the andromeda, amid the spruce. Its hum was heard afar at first, like that of a large bee, bringing a larger summer. This sight and sound would make me think I was in the tropics, — in Demerara or Maracaibo.

May 29, 1857. Soon I hear the low all-pervading hum of an approaching hummingbird circling above the rock, which afterward I mistake several times for the gruff voices of men approaching, unlike as these sounds are in some respects, and I perceive the resemblance even when I know better. Now I am sure it is a hummingbird, and now that it is two farmers approaching. But presently the hum becomes more sharp and thrilling, and the little fellow suddenly perches on an ash twig within a rod of me, and plumes himself while the rain is fairly beginning. He is quite out of proportion to the size of his perch. It does not acknowledge his weight.

— *Henry David Thoreau*

tobacco was used as a medicinal plant, the bird was known as the "doctor bird," a label it still carries in the islands. Some of the pueblo tribes also connected tobacco with the hummingbird. A Cochiti myth, for example, describes how the Mother, when she sent Hummingbird and Fly to get smoke in order to purify the earth, required them to visit Caterpillar, the guardian of the tobacco plant.

The symbol of the hummingbird is common on pueblo decorations and costumes. It is used on pottery, both old and new, with stylized forms, and dancers depict hummingbirds in some ceremonial rites. In the Hopi tradition, Tócha, the Hummingbird, is one of the principle kachinas, or spiritual figures. This kachina is represented by a green mask with a beak. The top of the head is yellow, a ruff of Douglas fir is worn by the dancer along with green moccasins, and the body is painted blue-green. Together, these colors represent the sky. At the Zuñi pueblo, Rain priests use hummingbird feathers in certain rituals; they are the only members of the tribe allowed to use feathers from this bird. Hopi fathers traditionally made special religious offerings, called road markers, in order to make their sons as swift as the hummingbird. These offerings included the wing feathers of the hummingbird tied to a long string.

At the Isleta pueblo, part of the Tiwa culture, hummingbirds are also part of a special ritual for stillborn children. In this culture, babies who die before they are four days old are believed to be reborn. To hasten the rebirth, prayer sticks with hummingbird feathers attached are used in a ceremony held before sunrise on the winter solstice, a time when the sun is also being born again, beginning its ascent to summer. After the arrival of Christianity, this traditional myth was also incorporated into at least one biblical myth, the rebirth of Christ, with hummingbirds representing the resurrection. In modern times, some Indian and Hispanic cultures in the southwest believe that hummingbirds are important protectors of the baby Jesus, holding up his diapers with their tiny bills.

Hummingbird designs on pre-Columbian pottery found in Peru and part of the Nasca culture (370 B.C.–540 A.D.).
(Drawn from a photograph in *Local Differences and Time Differences in Nasca Pottery*, by Donald A. Proulx, 1968, University of California Press.)

A myth from the Acoma pueblo relates how the volcano demon, who had lost a gambling game with the Sun's son, was blinded. In his blindness, raging fires were set to the piñon trees by his molten lava and many birds were burned while trying to put them out. The hummingbird flew to the great waters in the north, south, east, and west, gathering the clouds. Falling hail and rain then doused the fires, although nothing could relieve the heat. Because the tiny bird flew through the rainbow created by these clouds, he wore the colors of the rainbow on his throat.

Sacred medicine symbols among the Fox tribe included the hummingbird, which was carried in traveling bundles. Taken out of the pack and thrown, the bird gave the bearer special hummingbird-

HOW THEY BROUGHT BACK THE TOBACCO

In the beginning of the world, when people and animals were all the same, there was only one tobacco plant, to which they all came for their tobacco until Dagûl'kû, the geese, stole it and carried it far away to the south. The people were suffering without it, and there was one old woman who grew so thin and weak that everybody said she would soon die unless she could get tobacco to keep her alive. Different animals offered to go for it, one after another, the larger ones first and then the smaller ones, but the Dagûl'kû saw and killed every one before it could get to the plant. After the others the little Mole tried to reach it by going under the ground, but the Dagûl'kû saw his track and killed him as he came out. At last the Hummingbird offered to try. But the others said he was entirely too small and might as well stay at home. He begged them to let him try, so they showed him a plant in a field and told him to let them see how he would go about it. The next moment he was gone and they saw him sitting on the plant, and then in a moment he was back again, but no one had seen him going or coming, because he was so swift. "This is the way I'll do," said the Hummingbird, so they let him try. He flew off to the east, and when he came in sight of the tobacco the Dagûl'kû were watching all about it, but they could not see him because he was so small and flew so swiftly. He darted down on the plant — tsa! — and snatched off the top with the leaves and seeds, and was off again before the Dagûl'kû knew what had happened. Before he got home with the tobacco the old woman had fainted and they thought she was dead, but he blew the smoke into her nostrils, and with a cry of "Tsa'lu! [Tobacco!]" she opened her eyes and was alive again.

Myths of the Cherokee, 1897–98

like powers, including stealth and speed, useful when sneaking up on enemy villages. During battles, the bearer of hummingbird medicine was untouchable by enemy arrows unless the body of the hummingbird was itself hit. Hummingbird medicine could also be made from the heart of the bird that was ground up and mixed with other potent ingredients to make a powder that would protect the user against harm during an attack.

Other powers have also been attributed to hummingbirds. In Zuñi tradition, the sound of the hummingbird is a good omen, along with the sounds of the owl, and water in a stream. In Cuba, a traditional love potion is created from dried and powdered hummingbirds. In Puerto Rico, healers recommend the use of tea made from the burned ashes of hummingbird nests to cure asthma. Talismans made from hummingbird nests may also be worn on a string around the neck to cure this ailment.

At the Isleta Pueblo, one of the original Hopi cultures, hummingbird feathers are traditionally used on prayer-sticks used in some seasonal religious ceremonies. In some parts of the Caribbean, voodoo charms are made with hummingbird bodies to protect gardens and crops from thieves. A small piece taken from a hummingbird's nest, inserted into the ear, can be used to cure an earache, according to local folklore in the Dominican Republic. Also tradition in the Dominican Republic, hummingbird nests or material taken from them is sometimes used to stem the flow of blood in an open wound.

The Gê Indians of central Brazil have several myths relating to hummingbirds, often with the tiny birds performing special services. In one, a man who was sick had an ant crawl into his ear, biting into his flesh and holding on. A hummingbird flew to the man and used his long beak to pull the ant out of the man's ear. This man is then carried to the sky by a flock of vultures, where he gained special hunting powers. In another tale, an Indian burns his foot, which will not heal. Two hummingbirds appear at his hut and reveal that they are the spirits of his grandmother and grandfather. The birds place powdered leaves from a special tree on the injured foot, which the man rubs, pushing out a burning ember and ending his pain.

Other tribal tales from the Amazon basin tell of lost children who change into hummingbirds, flying away to become stars in the sky. Tribal religion from this region also includes the use of hummingbirds as symbolic elements in rituals. A special staff is used during a ceremony to connect the three levels of the universe — the sky, the human plane, and the earth. Hummingbird feathers decorate the

HUMMINGBIRD MAGIC

In parts of Mexico and South America today, some people believe that hummingbirds have special powers. Powder made from dried hummingbird bodies is used as an amulet, to attract romantic interest in the opposite sex and bring power and wealth. Powdered hummingbird — Polvo de Chuparrosa in Spanish — is sold in packets for use in rituals and is also commercially available premixed in colognes, perfumes, and special votive candles.

Line engraving of the Topaz hummingbird from *The Animal Kingdom Illustrated*, by Goodrich and Winchell, published in 1867.

staff as symbols of the masculine elements; when the staff is pushed into the ground, it connects with the feminine element in the earth, fertilizing it and allowing humans to be born. Another religious belief describes how the hummingbird, associated with the sun, carries the end of a vine to the sky, allowing the sun to rise in the sky.

Hummingbirds can represent the living souls of the dead, and a link to the flowers of the sacred tobacco plant. But hummingbirds can also represent less positive images to these tribes. These birds, members of species that are characteristically drab in color, are known to biologists as hermit hummingbirds, and to the Indians as tsíísanti, demons associated with the feminine and symbols of evil.

In some of the prehistoric Mexican cultures, the hummingbird was considered to be a transformed butterfly. In Zinacantecan mythology, an evil witch hummingbird flies at night, the opposite of the beneficial daytime hummingbird. The witch bird is responsible for spreading sickness and disease.

AZTEC HUMMINGBIRDS

"The humming-bird is the miracle of all our winged animals; he is feathered as a bird, and ghets his living as the bees, by sucking the honey from each flower."
— John Lawson, 1709

The hummingbird played a major role in the religion of the Aztecs in ancient Mexico. Huitzilopochtli was the most famous of all the Aztec gods during the final chapters of Aztec civilization, before the intrusion of Spanish explorers ended this long-running dynasty. Huitzilopochtli was originally a hunting god and as old as the beginnings of the Aztec empire, which is linked to the Mexica tribe. The Mexica tribe inhabited parts of northern Mexico for several centuries and migrated to Lake Tetzcoco about 1300 A.D. As the tribe grew, expanded its power, and united with other tribes to form the Aztec empire, Huitzilopochtli also grew in stature and importance, ultimately being elevated to the highest ranks of this civilization's religious deities.

Huitzilopochtli was portrayed with the head of a hummingbird fastened to the back of his head, or worn helmet-like. Some images of the god show his head with a helmet covered in hummingbird feathers. The hummingbird, in fact, is called huitzilin in the Nahuatl language that the Aztecs used. Huitzilopochtli's name stems from this word, as well as opochtli, the Nahuatl word for "left," so chosen because in the tradition of this religion, south was considered left and left was the direction of godly power. Thus, Huitzilopochtli was literally the "Hummingbird from the Left."

Aztec warriors were believed to be reincarnated as hummingbirds. When warriors died, their spirits were thought to first congregate around the sun; after four years, the spirits settled in the bodies of hummingbirds. Huitzilopochtli was born to Coatlicue, a goddess who conceived the child from a ball of hummingbird feathers that had fallen from the sky. Angry that their mother was pregnant illegitimately, Huitzilopochtli's brothers and sisters schemed to take her life. But just as they attacked her, Huitzilopochtli was born, fully formed and carrying a shield and spear, which he used to kill the attackers.

A suburban section of Mexico City known as Churubusco was originally the site known by the Aztecs as Huitzilopocho, or "Hummingbird Springs." Here, according to legend, sacrificial victims were ceremoniously bathed before being killed. Traditional Moche rituals include the use of a Hummingbird Staff, a rod decorated with hummingbird feathers and used to ritually "suck" evil objects from people who have been cursed by sorcerers. The Mochica also associated hummingbirds with battle, the fearless birds representing warriors. In some myths, hummingbirds also are messengers, swift runners able to outrace their opponents.

Hummingbird feathers were used by the Aztecs to adorn clothing worn by royalty and priests. On some capes used in religious ceremonies, feathers completely covered the outer surfaces. The hummingbird itself was considered an omen: when sighted it meant the coming of summer. In Aztec religion, the hummingbird literally

"Their beake is verye longe for the proportion of theyr bodies: and as fyne and subtile as a sowyng nedle. They are very hardye: so that when they see a man clyme the tree whee they haue thyr nestes, they flye at hys face and stryke him in the eyes, commyng, goynge, and retournynge with such swyftnes that no man woulde lightly beleue it that hath not seene it. And certenly these byrdes are so lyttle, that I durst not haue made mention hereof if it were not that diuers other which haue seen them as wel as I, can beare witnes of my saying."
— Ganzalo Fernandex de Oviedo y Valdez
(*Sumario de la Natural Historia de las Indias*, 1526)

represented the seasons of spring and summer, when the sun gradually rose in the sky, climbing from the south to the north. At this time, the hummingbirds, which were thought to hibernate, came alive again, bringing with them the rain and a rebirth of life. In one early document from 1653, relating the efforts of the Spanish to convert the natives to Christianity, priests borrowed this myth to help convince their reluctant audiences to switch to the new religion. In their "Christian" version, the hummingbirds' annual return in the spring was used as proof of the Resurrection. And even in modern times, Mexican folktales link hummingbirds with the baby Jesus, who is often pictured with these birds holding up his diapers.

Traditional designs for Hummingbird (Huitzizillin) used in the Aztec culture of ancient Mexico.
(Adapted from *Design Motifs of Ancient Mexico*, by Jorge Enciso, published by Dover Publications, 1953.)

THE LANGUAGE OF HUMMINGBIRDS

PUERTO RICO, DOMINICAN REPUBLIC *zumbador*

CUBA *zunzún, zum-zum*

HAITI *ouanga négresse*

FRENCH WEST INDIES *madère, bourdoneur, bourdons, murmures*

CREOLE *murmure, bourdon, frou-frou, fou-fou*

NAHUATL *huitzilin, pigada, ourbiri*
(literally "rays of the sun" and "tresses of the day star")

CAMPA-NOMATSIGUENGA (Amazon basin Indians) *tsopiti*

INCAN *ccenti*

MAYAN *ts'unu'un*

ZINACANTECAN *k'ochol pepen*

TAINO *colibri* or *cacique*

ANTILLES *murmures*

KUTENAI *nuktsáqteit*

SOUTH AMERICAN LOCAL DIALECTS *guanumbia, quinde, ourissa, huitizitzil, teominejo, chupaflor* ("flower sucker"), *beija flor* ("flower kisser"), *limpiacasa* ("house cleaner"), *chuparosa* ("rose sucker")

European explorers contributed some of the names used for hummingbirds, including the following ...

SPANISH *picaflor, colibri, paxaro mosquito, tominejo, cominejo*

PORTUGUESE *beija flor, colibri*

FRENCH *oiseau-mouche*

ITALIAN *colibri*

DUTCH *kolibrie, kolibrielje*

FINNISH, DANISH, GERMAN *kolibri*

AMERICAN INDIAN LANGUAGES

BILOXI *momoxka*

OSAGE *i'xthiwathe zhin-ga*

HOPI *to'tsa, pa'la to'tsa* (rufous), *sakwa'to'tsa* (blue-green)

APACHE *dátílyé*

NAVAJO *dah yiitjhí*

PIMA *na-na-tska*

WINTU *lutchi herit*

KAROK *hou-pu-chee-naish-wen*

CHOCTAW *liku^{n}klo*

SENECA *dzotháwendo^{n}*

THE BIRD THAT HUMS

Hummingbirds, as the name suggests, are named after the unique sound they make in flight, a hum sometimes confused with that of a bee. The word hum itself is originally from the Middle English language, the English as it was used from the twelfth to fifteenth centuries. The verb *hummen,* to hum, is also the same as in Middle High German, a form of the language originally used in the middle and central parts of that country. The scientific name for the hummingbird family is Trochilidae, a word originally borrowed from a bird known to the Greeks as a trochilus, which was commonly observed picking parasites from the open mouths of crocodiles. In the classic European languages — including French, Italian, German, and Spanish — no word for hummingbird existed until after the exploration of the New World began in the late 1400s.

NAMES

"That which we call the humming bird, much less than a Wren, not much bigger than an humble Bee ... never sitting, but purring with her wings, all the time she stayes with the flower." — R. Ligon, 1657

ALLEN'S HUMMINGBIRD *Selasphorus sasin.* Named for Charles A. Allen (1841–1930), an amateur ornithologist who is credited with being the first to recognize this bird as a distinct species. The Allen's Hummingbird had previously been considered the same as the rufous. The roots of the word Selasphorus, created by William Swainson in 1831, are from the Greek. Selas means "light," and phorus means "carrying," hence the translation, light carrier, or torchbearer. The species name Sasin was chosen by Rene Lesson. Some sources explain that he choose the word from a French translation of a book about the third voyage of Captain Cook; other sources believe the name was adapted from the Nootka Indian word for hummingbird. Lesson first described this bird in 1829.

ANNA'S HUMMINGBIRD *Calypte anna.* Named for Anna de Belle Massena, the Princess of Rivoli (1806–circa 1896). Her husband, Francois Massena, the Duke of Rivoli, was the inspiration for the name of Rivoli's Hummingbird (a.k.a. the Magnificent Hummingbird). Rene Lesson, an important naturalist at the time, picked this name for the species in 1829 because of the Princess Anna's noted beauty. John Gould assigned the scientific name for the genus in 1856. The word Calypte comes from the Greek kalyptos, meaning "hidden."

BERYLLINE HUMMINGBIRD *Amazilia beryllina.* Named for the color of beryl, a naturally-occurring metallic element that is typically aqua, turquoise, or blue-green. The scientific name was created by Rene Lesson, who first described the genus in 1843 and chose the name Amazili from a South American tribal word for Amazon River region.

BLACK-CHINNED HUMMINGBIRD *Archilochus alexandri*. Named for the distinctive black patch under the beak and extending to the sides of the head. The name Archilochus is from the Greek; arch is used as a prefix and means "chief," and lochos means "a body of people." Archilochus in this context was created to mean "first among the birds." Archilochus was also the name of an ancient Greek poet, whose poetry was dedicated to a beautiful maiden. Jules Bourcier and Martial Etienne Mulsant, French naturalists, were the first to publish a description of the black-chinned hummingbird, which they observed in Sierra Madre, Mexico. They attributed the name, alexandri, to a Dr. M. Alexandre, who is credited with first sighting this bird in 1846, but no record exists of who he was.

BLUE-THROATED HUMMINGBIRD *Lampornis clemenciae*. Named for the bright blue color of its chin patch. The scientific name comes from the Greek words lampas, or "lamp," and ornis, for "bird." Clemenciae is a derivation of Clemence, the first name of the wife of Rene Lesson (1794–1849), a French naturalist who first described this bird in 1829.

BROAD-BILLED HUMMINGBIRD *Cynanthus latirostris*. Named for the wider-than-normal bill. William Swainson (1789–1855), was a naturalist who received credit for first describing this genus; he published his findings in 1827. Cynanthus includes the root anthos, a Greek word meaning "flower," and kynos, meaning "dog" (or kyanos, dark blue and anthos, bright). Latirostris is a derivative of the Greek words meaning "wide" or "broad" and "bill."

BROAD-TAILED HUMMINGBIRD *Selasphorus platycercus*. Named for its broad tail structure. The roots of the word Selasphorus are from the Greek: selas means "light," and phorus means "carrying," hence the translation light carrier, or torchbearer. The root word platys in Greek means "broad" or "flat" and cercus is a version of kerkos, Greek for "tail." William Swainson first described this genus in 1831, and he coined the name.

BUFF-BELLIED HUMMINGBIRD *Amazilia yucatanensis*. Named for the brownish color of its belly. Yucatanensis means, literally in the formal Greek style, "from the Yucatan." The bird was first described in 1898 by Dr. Harry Oberholser, an ornithologist who worked for the U.S. Fish and Wildlife Service and later was Curator

Selasphorus rufus.

Woodcut illustration of a rufous hummingbird from
A History of North American Birds, by Baird, Brewer, and Ridgway,
published by Little, Brown, & Company in 1874.

of Ornithology at the Cleveland Museum of Natural History. He made his observations from a specimen captured near Brownsville, Texas, a location then known as Beeville.

CALLIOPE HUMMINGBIRD *Stellula calliope*. Named by John Gould (1804–1881), a prominent English ornithologist. The bird was named after Calliope, one of the nine daughters of Zeus and Mnemosyne, who were the nine muses of ancient Greek mythology and traditionally considered patrons of the arts. Calliope was the muse assigned to epic poetry and eloquence. Stellula in Latin refers to a small star. Gould first described the Calliope in 1847.

COSTA'S HUMMINGBIRD *Calypte costae*. Named for the Marquis de Beauregard, whose legal name was Louis Marie Pantaleon Costa (1806–1864). Costa had a fascination with hummingbirds and developed an extensive collection of specimens. The name was assigned in 1839 by Jule Bourcier, a French naturalist, who found and described the first specimen which was from Baja California.

LUCIFER HUMMINGBIRD *Calothorax lucifer*. Named after the archangel Lucifer, also known as the bearer of light, the torchbearer, and the morning star. In Greek, Calothoras comes from calos, meaning "beautiful," and thorax, or "chest." The Calothorax genus was originally described by G. R. Gray (1808–1872), an English ornithologist who created this scientific name in 1840. The Lucifer Hummingbird species was first described by William Swainson in 1827.

MAGNIFICENT HUMMINGBIRD (formerly known as Rivoli's Hummingbird) *Eugenes fulgens*. Originally named after the Duke of Rivoli, Francois Victor Massena (1799–1863). Rivoli was noted for his patronage of natural history and particularly the study of birds. The Greek name Eugenes means "of good breeding" or "well born." Fulgens means "glittering." John Gould first described this bird in 1856.

HUMMINGBIRD SITES

Geographical locations in the United States named for the hummingbird include:

- one CANYON (in Arizona)
- twelve SPRINGS (five in Arizona, three in California, and one each in New Mexico, Nevada, Oregon, and Utah)
- six CREEKS (four in California, one each in Montana and Oregon)
- four LAKES (two in California, one each in Georgia and Michigan)
- one PEAK (in Montana)
- one BASIN (in Montana)
- one GAP (in New Mexico)
- one MOUNTAIN (in Oregon)

RUBY-THROATED HUMMINGBIRD *Archilochus colubris*. Named for the bright ruby patch on its throat. The name Archilochus is from the Greek; arch is used as a prefix and means "chief," and lochos means "a body of people." Archilochus in this context was created to mean "first among the birds." In Greek, colubris means "serpent," and is considered by some scientists to be so inappropriate that it may have been a misspelling by its original namer, who could have been attempting to derive a word from the French name for hummingbird, "colibre." Carl Linneaus, the father of modern scientific classification, gets this credit; he first described the genus in 1758, from a specimen collected in South Carolina.

RUFOUS HUMMINGBIRD *Selasphorus rufus*. Named for the rufous, or reddish color of its head and body. The scientific name is translated from the Latin as "rufous flame bearer." The species was first described in 1788 by Johann Gmelin (1709–1755), a German explorer who spotted the first bird on Vancouver Island, British Columbia.

VIOLET-CROWNED HUMMINGBIRD *Amazilia violiceps.* Named for the violet cap of color on its head. Violiceps is a combination of Greek words meaning "violet" and "head." The bird was first described by Hans von Berlepsch in 1889, and originally named Amazilia verticalis. Berlepsch was a German ornithologist, an honorary fellow of the American Ornithologists Union, and a leading authority on the birds of South America.

WHITE-EARED HUMMINGBIRD *Hylocharis leucotis.* The scientific name Hylocharis comes from the Greek words hyle, "woods,"

Line engraving from *Illustrations Typographiques,*
a catalog of illustrations for printers published
in France by Henri-Désiré Porret in 1842.

and charis, "beauty." The Greek word for "white" is leukos. Ludlow Griscom, an American ornithologist prominent in the early 1900s, is credited with first describing this bird in 1929.

XÁNTUS' HUMMINGBIRD *Hylocharis xantusii.* Named for John Xántus, a naturalist who lived from 1825 to 1894. George Newbold Lawrence (1806–1895), a noted amateur ornithologist, is credited with first descriptions of 70 bird species. He named this bird for Xántus, first describing it in 1860. Xántus was born in Hungary, but immigrated to the United States when he was twenty-five.

GROUP OF HUMMING-BIRDS.

Line engraving from *Cecil's Books of Natural History*, by Selim Peabody, published by American Book Exchange in 1886.

HUMMINGBIRD SPECIES

NOTE: *Additional species of hummingbirds that are occasional visitors to North America are listed on page 162.*

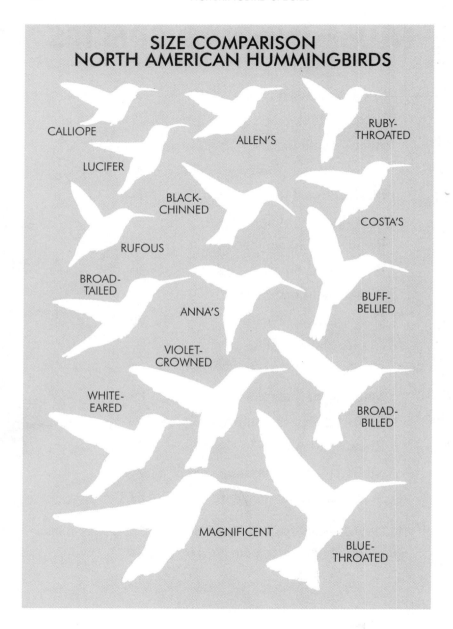

SIZE COMPARISON
NORTH AMERICAN HUMMINGBIRDS

CALLIOPE

ALLEN'S

RUBY-
THROATED

LUCIFER

BLACK-
CHINNED

COSTA'S

RUFOUS

BROAD-
TAILED

ANNA'S

BUFF-
BELLIED

VIOLET-
CROWNED

WHITE-
EARED

BROAD-
BILLED

MAGNIFICENT

BLUE-
THROATED

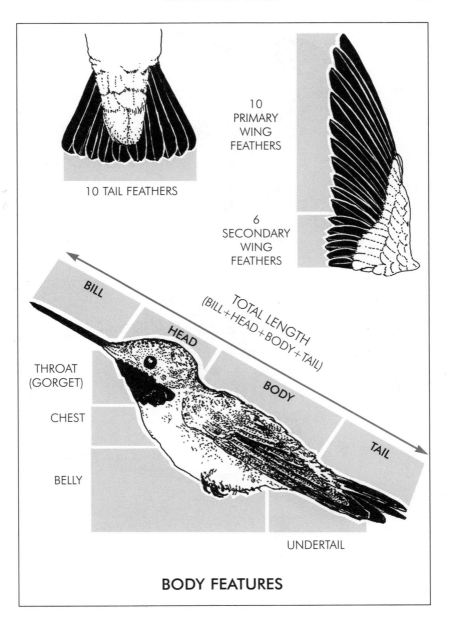

10 TAIL FEATHERS

10 PRIMARY WING FEATHERS

6 SECONDARY WING FEATHERS

BILL

HEAD

TOTAL LENGTH
(BILL+HEAD+BODY+TAIL)

THROAT (GORGET)

BODY

CHEST

TAIL

BELLY

UNDERTAIL

BODY FEATURES

ALLEN'S HUMMINGBIRD
FEMALE

ALLEN'S HUMMINGBIRD
MALE

VITAL STATISTICS

OFFICIAL NAME	Allen's hummingbird *Selasphorus sasin*
COMMON NAMES	Red-backed hummingbird Spanish: chupamirto petirrojo
DESCRIPTION	One of the smallest N.A. hummingbirds. Reddish-brown or rufous color on the sides of the chest and tail (but not on the back). The bill is straight and dark colored. The tail is pointed when folded. Males slightly smaller than females. **MALE** Chin and throat scarlet, red, or orange; head and back metallic green with bronze tones; sides of head brown or rufous; upper chest white; sides and abdomen tan or rufous; tail brown or rufous, including underneath; wing feathers dark brown or dark gray. **FEMALE** Back green or bronze-green; throat may be spotted with metallic colors similar to the male; tail may have brown or rufous tones; chest and abdomen white, or white mixed with brown; white tips on outside tail feathers.
COMPARISON	Similar to rufous hummingbird, except for color of head and back, which are metallic green. Immature males and females identical to the rufous.

TOTAL LENGTH	3.3–3.75" 84–95 mm	**WING LENGTH**	1.5" 37–39 mm
WEIGHT	.09–.13 oz 2.5–3.8 gm	**TAIL**	short, forked
		BILL LENGTH	.59–.67" 15–17 mm

RANGE	Permanent colonies found in southern California, in Los Angeles County and in the Channel Islands. Migratory birds found January–October from California north to southern Oregon, from the coast inland to the Sierras. Winter range is western half of Mexico, including Baja California. Migration path includes extreme southern Arizona. Occasional sightings along the Gulf Coast from Texas to Louisiana and in western Washington.
HABITAT	Open or partly wooded areas, including brushy slopes, canyons, willow and dogwood thickets, live oak stands, and chaparral, mostly within the range of coastal fog.
FOOD	California fuchsia, honeysuckle, Indian paintbrush, madrone, monkey-flower, other flowering shrubs.
BREEDING	Mating: late winter to early spring. Nesting often in trees in shaded conditions; nest often camouflaged with lichen or pieces of bark. 2 eggs; incubation 17–22 days. First feathers: about 7 days. First flight: 22–25 days.
VOCAL CALL	Brief, non-musical "chip, chip, chip."
HABITS	Very territorial, with males defending both feeding and mating zones. Chases insects in the air. Male dives in steep "J" pattern during aggressive or mating displays, bobbing tail at bottom of arc. During normal flight, the tail is held in a high position. Competes with Anna's hummingbirds.

RANGE OF ALLEN'S HUMMINGBIRD

Represents traditional range of species, including some migratory areas. Expansion of range may include more territory within states than is indicated.

● Represents states where species is also occasionally sighted.

Represents normal migratory area outside of breeding territory.

ANNA'S HUMMINGBIRD
FEMALE

ANNA'S HUMMINGBIRD
MALE

VITAL STATISTICS

OFFICIAL NAME	Anna's hummingbird *Calypte anna*
COMMON NAMES	Spanish: Chupamirto cuello escarlata
DESCRIPTION	Large hummingbird. Green back and red throat and head. Bill is straight and dark-colored. Tail of medium length and slightly forked when folded; tail held level with body when hovering. Males and females about the same size. **MALE** Chin and throat metallic violet or red; head metallic violet or red except for green patch behind eyes and back of head; back, upper tail, and upper wings metallic green; chest off-white to gray with green streaks or patches on sides; white tuft on either side of tail; under-tail area has white or gray borders. **FEMALE** Green back and head; white or gray chest and abdomen; throat features small patch of metallic red; outside tail feathers have white tips.
COMPARISON	Only N.A. hummingbird with red head. Males and females lack any rufous coloring.

TOTAL LENGTH	3.5–4" 89–101 mm	**WING LENGTH**	1.9–2" 48–51 mm
WEIGHT	.12–.2 ozs 3.3–5.8 gm	**TAIL**	long, forked
		BILL LENGTH	.67–.87" 17–22 mm

RANGE	Permanent resident of California, extreme southern Nevada, most of Arizona, southern New Mexico, and northern Mexico. Seasonal in Oregon, Washington and western Nevada. Occasional sightings in Gulf states east to Florida.
HABITAT	Forests, chapparal, scrubland, canyons, mountain slopes.
FOOD	Red gooseberry, red-flowering currant, fuchsias, tree tobacco, blue-curl, monkey flower, Indian pink, Indian paintbrush, century plant, eucalyptus, insects on tree bark, tree sap.
BREEDING	Mating: December–June. Nesting from 3–30 feet above ground in vines, shrubs, or trees; nests up to 50 mm wide, constructed largely from fibers and covered with lichens. 2 eggs; incubation 14–19 days. First flight: 18–23 days. In most of its range has two broods per season.
VOCAL CALL	Sharp, clipped "chip, chip, chip" from males and females when feeding. During courting, males have song pattern of short treble notes.
HABITS	Very territorial, with females sometimes also defending feeding sites. Hunts for insects on tree trunks and feeds on tree sap. Mating behavior of males includes steep dives with sharp vocal call at bottom of dive and back-and-forth "shuttle" flights in front of perched females. May be found with Allen's and rufous hummingbirds. Common in urban areas.

RANGE OF ANNA'S HUMMINGBIRD

Represents traditional range of species, including some migratory areas. Expansion of range may include more territory within states than is indicated.

● Represents states where species is also occasionally sighted.

Represents normal migratory area outside of breeding territory.

BLACK-CHINNED
HUMMINGBIRD
FEMALE

BLACK-CHINNED
HUMMINGBIRD
MALE

VITAL STATISTICS

OFFICIAL NAME	Black-chinned hummingbird *Archilochus alexandri*
COMMON NAMES	purple-throated hummingbird Spanish: terciopelo barbanegro
DESCRIPTION	Medium-sized hummingbird. Metallic green back and head. Long, straight dark bill. Tail features notch when folded. Males smaller than females. **MALE** Chin and throat black with metallic purple on lower part; head and back metallic green; sides of head and behind eyes black; chest white to gray or light brown; sides streaked with metallic green or bronze-green; under-tail brown or gray with white borders; white tufts on sides of tail base. **FEMALE** Back, upper wings, and upper tail dull metallic green; head darker and duller in color; chest and abdomen white to gray; outer tail feathers have white tips; wings darker in color.
COMPARISON	Similar to Costa and Lucifer hummingbirds, but Costa lacks green color on head and Lucifer features unique long, protruding feathers on throat.

TOTAL LENGTH	3.3–3.75" 84–95 mm	**WING LENGTH**	1.6–1.7" 41–44 mm
WEIGHT	.09–.14 oz. 2.7–4.1 gm	**TAIL**	short, forked
		BILL LENGTH	.71–.83" 18–21 mm

RANGE	Migratory birds found March–September. Breeds from eastern Washington and British Columbia south, including parts of Idaho, Oregon, California, Nevada, Utah, western Colorado, Arizona, New Mexico, and Texas. Occasionally found in Gulf states east to Florida. Winter range is northern Mexico.
HABITAT	Meadows in mountainous areas, forests, canyons, chapparal, desert washes. Common in cultivated fields and orchards, including irrigated areas.
FOOD	Small flying insects, ocotillo, agave, honeysuckle, tree tobacco, cultivated citrus trees, palo verde, ironweed, mountain laurel, and many others.
BREEDING	Mating: early to late spring. Nesting 3–10 feet above ground, usually in tree forks; nests typically made from yellowish fiber from Sycamore leaves. 2 eggs: incubation 13–16 days. First flight: about 21 days.
VOCAL CALL	Not very vocal; call is low-pitched, soft "tchew."
HABITS	Male dives in steep arcs and tight "shuttle" flights while courting. Males and females fan and pump their tails rapidly while hovering. May chase flying insects. Found in the same areas as Costa's hummingbird; overlapping range with ruby-throated hummingbird in Texas only.

RANGE OF BLACK-CHINNED HUMMINGBIRD

Represents traditional range of species, including some migratory areas. Expansion of range may include more territory within states than is indicated.

● Represents states where species is also occasionally sighted.

Represents normal migratory area outside of breeding territory.

**BLUE-THROATED
HUMMINGBIRD**
FEMALE

**BLUE-THROATED
HUMMINGBIRD**
MALE

VITAL STATISTICS

OFFICIAL NAME	Blue-throated hummingbird *Lampornis clemenciae*
COMMON NAMES	Spanish: Chupamirto garganta azul
DESCRIPTION	One of the largest hummingbirds in North America. Metallic green on back and head. Bill long, straight and dark. Tail somewhat squared in males. Males larger than females. **MALE** Chin and throat metallic blue; head, back, chest, and abdomen dull metallic green; white markings behind and below eyes; tail dark green with distinctive white edges and tips on outermost feathers; under tail area has white edges; white tufts at base and sides of tail. **FEMALE** Coloring similar to male but without distinctive blue patch on chin and throat; chest and abodomen brown to dark gray; tail dark green with distinctive white edges and tips on outermost feathers.
COMPARISON	Only similar hummingbird in North America is Rivoli's hummingbird, but blue-throated hummingbird has white markings on tail and is larger of the two.

TOTAL LENGTH	4.5–5.25" 114–133 mm	**WING LENGTH**	2.7–3.1" 68–80 mm
WEIGHT	.28 oz 8 gm	**TAIL**	long, forked
		BILL LENGTH	.87–.98" 22–25 mm

RANGE	Southeastern Arizona, southwestern New Mexico, and southwestern Texas, south through central Mexico to central America. Winters in central Mexico. Occasional sightings north to Colorado and Utah and east to Louisiana.
HABITAT	Prefers wooded areas near streams, dense canyon vegetation, desert mountains.
FOOD	Penstemon, tree tobacco, lobelia, cardinal flower, agave, sage, insects, spiders.
BREEDING	Mating: April–June. Nesting often in covered areas such as overhanging rocks; nests are large and bulky for hummingbirds; nests made from plant material and attached at the side or rim. 2 eggs; incubation 17–18 days. First flight: 24–29 days.
VOCAL CALL	Loud, high-pitched "seep." Calls in flight, while feeding and perching.
HABITS	Very aggressive and territorial. Feeds heavily on insects. Competes with Rivoli, violet-crowned, magnificent, and black-chinned hummingbirds. Males and females frequently spread tail feathers.

ARIZONA

NEW
MEXICO

TEXAS

RANGE OF BLUE-THROATED HUMMINGBIRD

Represents traditional range of species, including some migratory areas. Expansion of range may include more territory within states than is indicated.

● Represents states where species is also occasionally sighted.

Represents normal migratory area outside of breeding territory.

BROAD-BILLED
HUMMINGBIRD
FEMALE

BROAD-BILLED
HUMMINGBIRD
MALE

VITAL STATISTICS

OFFICIAL NAME	Broad-billed hummingbird *Cynanthus latirostris*
COMMON NAMES	Spanish: chupaflor piquiancho
DESCRIPTION	Large hummingbird. Metallic green back and head. Bill is long and straight and brightly colored in red. Tail is dark, long, and spiky. Males and females about same size. **MALE** Chin and throat metallic blue; head and back metallic green to bronze-green, head may be darker in color; may have paler patch behind eye; chest, sides, and abdomen same metallic green as back; tail dark, under tail white or gray at base; white tufts on sides of tail at base. **FEMALE** Head, back, sides, and abdomen dull metallic green; head may be duller in color or be more brown or grayish; white or gray spot behind eye; white tufts on sides of tail at base; bill dark but usually has reddish or pink color at base.
COMPARISON	White-eared hummingbird similar, has red bill, but also features distinct white marking behind eye, whiter and larger than in broad-billed.

TOTAL LENGTH	3.25–4" 83–101 mm	**WING LENGTH**	1.9–2.2" 49–57 mm
WEIGHT	.11–.16 oz 3.2–4.4 gm	**TAIL**	long, rounded
		BILL LENGTH	.75–.87" 19–22 mm

RANGE	Southern Arizona, southwestern New Mexico, southwestern Texas south to southern Mexico. Migratory birds found March–September. Winters in central Mexico. Rare sightings in California and Louisiana.
HABITAT	Rocky canyons and desert canyons near streams or springs.
FOOD	Ocotillo, Indian paintbrush, agaves, penstemons, century plant, tree tobacco, insects.
BREEDING	Mating: January–August. May have two broods in one season. Nesting low to ground; very small nests; nests made of plant material, leaves, and flower blossoms. 2 eggs; incubation about 14 days. First flight: 21–22 days.
VOCAL CALL	Loud, raspy "jedit."
HABITS	Male flies back and forth in a shallow arc during courtship, producing loud, high-pitched buzzing with wings. During flight, tail is flicked frequently while hovering.

RANGE OF BROAD-BILLED HUMMINGBIRD

Represents traditional range of species, including some migratory areas. Expansion of range may include more territory within states than is indicated.

● Represents states where species is also occasionally sighted.

Represents normal migratory area outside of breeding territory.

BROAD-TAILED
HUMMINGBIRD
FEMALE

BROAD-TAILED
HUMMINGBIRD
MALE

VITAL STATISTICS

OFFICIAL NAME	Broad-tailed hummingbird *Selasphorus platycercus*
COMMON NAMES	Spanish: Chupamirto cola ancha
DESCRIPTION	Medium-sized hummingbird. Metallic green back and head, ruby throat, some green coloring on sides. Long, dark bill. Long, wide tail, square at bottom. Males and females about same size. **MALE** Chin and throat bright metallic red; head and back metallic green to bronze-green; upper chest white to gray, lower chest and abdomen gray to brown; middle tail feathers metallic green, outer tail feather dark; wings brown to dark gray. **FEMALE** Chin and throat white to off-white; chest and abdomen buff to gray; white tips on outer tail feathers.
COMPARISON	Similar to calliope hummingbird, but calliope smaller and has white streaks on throat. Similar to ruby-throated hummingbird, but ruby-throated has shorter tail with distinct notch.

TOTAL LENGTH	4–4.5" 101–114 mm	**WING LENGTH**	1.8–2" 46–51 mm
WEIGHT	.09–.14 oz 2.5–4.1 gm	**TAIL**	long, square
		BILL LENGTH	.63–.75" 16–19 mm

RANGE	Migratory birds found March–September in Central Idaho, eastern California, southeastern Oregon, Nevada, Utah, western Wyoming, Colorado, Arizona, New Mexico, and western Texas south to Central America. Winters in central and southern Mexico. Occasional sightings in Gulf states east to Alabama.
HABITAT	Open wooded areas and meadows in mountains, principally aspen, piñon, juniper, and oak stands near streams.
FOOD	Mint, bouvardia, columbine, penstemon, delphinium, agave, yucca, ocotillo, figworts, gooseberry, ants, aphids, and other small insects.
BREEDING	Mating: spring months. Nests often found in trees; nests of plant fibers; outer surface of nest may be camouflages with lichens or pieces of bark. 2 eggs; incubation 16–19 days. First flight: 18–26 days.
VOCAL CALL	Musical high-pitched "chirp" or "chip."
HABITS	Very territorial. Males use high perches to survey territory. Male dives in "U" pattern during courtship, with hover at top of dive. Wings "hum" louder than other N.A. hummingbirds.

RANGE OF BROAD-TAILED HUMMINGBIRD

▓ Represents traditional range of species, including some
migratory areas. Expansion of range may include more territory
within states than is indicated.

● Represents states where species is also occasionally sighted.

▓ Represents normal migratory area outside of breeding territory.

BUFF-BELLIED
HUMMINGBIRD
FEMALE

BUFF-BELLIED
HUMMINGBIRD
MALE

VITAL STATISTICS

OFFICIAL NAME	Buff-bellied hummingbird *Amazilia yucatanensis*
COMMON NAMES	fawn-breasted hummingbird, Yucatan hummingbird. Spanish: chupamirto yucateco
DESCRIPTION	Large hummingbird. Metallic green back and head. Bill long, curved slightly down, wider at base, and distinctive red color, darker toward tip. Long tail colored reddish brown, slightly forked. Male and female similar in coloration. Males slightly larger than females. **MALE** Chin and throat metallic yellow-green; back metallic green to bronze-green; head darker; slight ring of buff around eye; upper chest same metallic yellow-green as chin and throat; lower chest and abdomen buff or brown; tail reddish brown; wing feathers dark. **FEMALE** Same coloring as male.
COMPARISON	May be confused with rufous hummingbird because of similar tail color, but rufous has red throat, white chest, and dark bill.

TOTAL LENGTH	4–4.5" 101–114 mm	**WING LENGTH**	2–2.3" 51–58 mm
WEIGHT	.11–.18 oz 3–5 gms	**TAIL**	long, forked
		BILL LENGTH	.75–.83" 19–21 mm

RANGE	Migratory birds found spring–fall in southern Texas and along Gulf coast of Texas south through Gulf regions of Mexico and Yucatan pennisula. Winters in Gulf regions of Mexico and Yucatan peninsula. Occasional sightings along Gulf coast east to Louisiana and north to central Texas.
HABITAT	Scrub areas and open woodlands, especially arroyos land near streams. Also found in cultivated areas, including gardens and orchards.
FOOD	Mesquite, Texas ebony, anaqua, giant Turk's cap.
BREEDING	Mating: March–July. Nesting close to ground; nests made from plant fibers; outside camouflaged with lichens and pieces of bark. 2 eggs: incubation period unknown. First flight: unknown.
VOCAL CALL	Several musical notes descending in pitch, uttered infrequently.
HABITS	Territorial. Flight is characterized by louder hum than most other hummingbirds in North America, also frequently flies in staccato, irregular pattern.

RANGE OF BUFF-BELLIED HUMMINGBIRD

Represents traditional range of species, including some migratory areas. Expansion of range may include more territory within states than is indicated.

● Represents states where species is also occasionally sighted.

Represents normal migratory area outside of breeding territory.

CALLIOPE HUMMINGBIRD
FEMALE

CALLIOPE HUMMINGBIRD
MALE

VITAL STATISTICS

OFFICIAL NAME	Calliope hummingbird *Stellula calliope*
COMMON NAMES	Spanish: chupamirto rafaguitas
DESCRIPTION	Smallest hummingbird in North America. Back and head metallic green. Short tail square across tips. Bill short, dark, and straight. Males smaller than females. **MALE** Chin and throat metallic dark red to purple, with some feathers distinctively long and narrow and some may feature white longitudinal stripes; head and back metallic green; chest white to gray; sides and abdomen off white, gray, or light brown, sometimes with slight green tinge; tail and wing feathers dark. **FEMALE** Chin and throat white; head and back metallic green to bronze-green; chest and abdomen white to gray; white tips on outer tail feathers.
COMPARISON	Similar to broad-tailed hummingbird, but smaller in size; broad-tailed without distinctive white striping on chin and throat patch.

TOTAL LENGTH	2.8–3.5" 71–89 mm	**WING LENGTH**	1.5–1.6" 37–40 mm
WEIGHT	.07–.11 oz 1.9–3.2 gm	**TAIL**	short, squared
		BILL LENGTH	.55–.59" 14–15 mm

RANGE	Migratory birds found March–September in British Columbia and western Alberta south through Washington, Idaho, western Montana, western Wyoming, Oregon, northern and eastern California, Nevada, and northwestern Utah. Winters in central Mexico. Occasional sightings in Colorado and Gulf states from Texas to Florida.
HABITAT	Meadows and conifer or hardwood forests in mountainous areas up to 10,000 feet, brushy canyons.
FOOD	Penstemon, gooseberry, currant, columbine, manzanita, monkey flower, lousewort, Indian paintbrush, snowplan, small flying insects.
BREEDING	Mating: May–June. Nesting sites protected by foliage; often nests in conifers with nest among pine cones; outer nest often camouflaged with lichens. 2 eggs: incubation 15–16 days. First flight: 18–23 days.
VOCAL CALL	Quiet, short nonmusical "tsip" and soft squeaks.
HABITS	Very territorial, may chase away larger hummingbird species. Chases insects in flight. Male dives in "U" pattern during courtship, with vocal call at bottom of dive. Tail held high and still when hovering.

RANGE OF CALLIOPE HUMMINGBIRD

Represents traditional range of species, including some
migratory areas. Expansion of range may include more territory
within states than is indicated.

● Represents states where species is also occasionally sighted.

Represents normal migratory area outside of breeding territory.

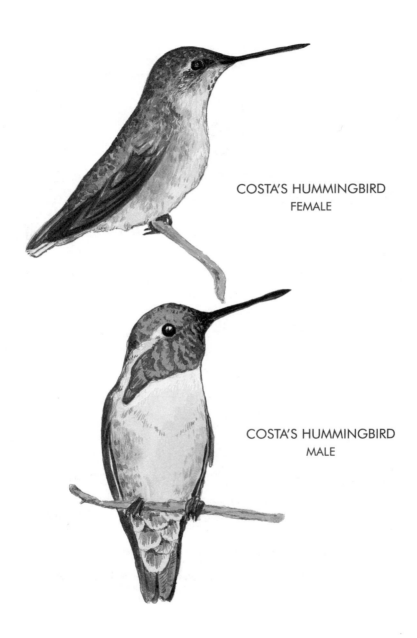

COSTA'S HUMMINGBIRD
FEMALE

COSTA'S HUMMINGBIRD
MALE

VITAL STATISTICS

OFFICIAL NAME	Costa's hummingbird *Calypte costae*
COMMON NAMES	coast hummingbird, ruffed hummingbird, Spanish: chupamirto garganta
DESCRIPTION	Medium-sized hummingbird. Metallic green head and back with metallic purple chin and throat. Bill is dark and straight. Tail is short and has shallow fork. Males and females about the same size. **MALE** Chin, throat, and head metallic purple; long feathers extend from throat into chest; back dull metallic green; streaks of white behind eyes; chest white; abdomen and sides gray with tinge of green; white under tail at base; feathers on tail and wings dark. **FEMALE** Chin and throat white; back dull metallic green; head darker; chest and abdomen white to gray; white tips on outer tail feathers.
COMPARISON	Male similar to Anna's hummingbird, except for purple color on head and throat and longer feathers on throat. Female very similar to female black-chinned and ruby-throated hummingbirds.

TOTAL LENGTH	3–3.5" 76–89 mm	**WING LENGTH**	1.7–1.8" 43–46 mm
WEIGHT	.09–.18 oz 2.5–5 gm	**TAIL**	long, forked
		BILL LENGTH	.63–.75" 16–19 mm

RANGE	Permanent colonies in southeastern California. Migratory birds from January–October in southern California, southern Nevada, and western Arizona south to Baja California and northwestern Mexico. Occasional sightings in New Mexico, Utah, northern California, Oregon, and Texas.
HABITAT	Desert and arid areas away from water sources, including arroyos, dry washes, and mesas; foothills, chaparral, low mountains.
FOOD	Ocotillo, mesquite, chuparosa, desert willow, tree tobacco, box thorn, desert lavender, desert willow, sage, larkspur, small insects.
BREEDING	Mating: April–March. Nesting in trees, shrubs, or cacti; nest usually low to ground; nests vary in size; made from plant fibers, leaves, bark, and lichens. 2 eggs; incubation 15–18 days. First flight: 20–23 days.
VOCAL CALL	Soft high-pitched "chip" and musical whistle.
HABITS	Territorial, with males using high perches for observation. Male dives in steep "U" pattern from high positions, with whistle at bottom of dive; also circles in horizontal plane during courtship. While hovering, males and females pump tails up and down. Favored habitats often have no source of water.

RANGE OF COSTA'S HUMMINGBIRD

Represents traditional range of species, including some migratory areas. Expansion of range may include more territory within states than is indicated.

● Represents states where species is also occasionally sighted.

Represents normal migratory area outside of breeding territory.

LUCIFER HUMMINGBIRD
FEMALE

LUCIFER HUMMINGBIRD
MALE

VITAL STATISTICS

OFFICIAL NAME	Lucifer hummingbird *Calothorax lucifer*
COMMON NAMES	Spanish: chupamirto morada grande
DESCRIPTION	Small-sized hummingbird. Metallic green back and head. Bill is long, dark, and curves slightly down. Tail is long and has a deep fork when folded. Males smaller than females. **MALE** Chin and throat metallic purple or violet, purple area extends to sides of head and throat feathers very long; head and back metallic green; chest white; abdomen and sides white to gray or buff; tail dark; wings dark. **FEMALE** Chin and throat white to gray; dark patch behind eye; abdomen and sides buff or gray; white tips on outer tail feathers.
COMPARISON	Male similar to Costa's and black-chinned hummingbirds, but Lucifer has forked tail, purple throat patch extends to sides, and no purple on head.

TOTAL LENGTH	3.5–3.75" 89–95 mm	**WING LENGTH**	1.4–1.5" 36–39 mm
WEIGHT	.08–.12 oz 2.2–3.3 gm	**TAIL**	long, forked
		BILL LENGTH	.79–.87" 20–22 mm

RANGE	Migratory birds found March–November in southwestern Texas and southeastern New Mexico south through central Mexico. Winters in central Mexico. Occasional sightings elsewhere in Texas and New Mexico, and Arizona.
HABITAT	Desert plateaus, mountain slopes.
FOOD	Ocotillo, agaves, bluebonnet, tree tobacco, penstemon, honeysuckle, century plant, insects.
BREEDING	Mating: May–July. Nesting in cacti or shrubs; nests made from plant fibers, leaves, and flowers. 2 eggs; incubation 15 days. First flight: 21–24 days.
VOCAL CALL	Quiet high-pitched "tick, tick, tick."
HABITS	Males and females territorial. During courtship, male flies back and forth shuttle flights in front of female after she has built a nest and while she is in it, diving in a steep pattern. Males also have zigzag flight with spread tail feathers.

RANGE OF LUCIFER HUMMINGBIRD

Represents traditional range of species, including some migratory areas. Expansion of range may include more territory within states than is indicated.

● Represents states where species is also occasionally sighted.

Represents normal migratory area outside of breeding territory.

MAGNIFICENT
HUMMINGBIRD
FEMALE

MAGNIFICENT
HUMMINGBIRD
MALE

VITAL STATISTICS

OFFICIAL NAME	Magnificent hummingbird *Eugenes fulgens*
COMMON NAMES	Rivoli's hummingbird, Spanish: chupaflor magnifico
DESCRIPTION	Large hummingbird. Darker metallic green than other hummingbirds, with dark chest. Dark tail with slight notch when folded. Bill is long, straight, and dark. Males larger than females. **MALE** Chin and throat metallic emerald green; back metallic green; head metallic purple or violet; small white patch behind eye; upper chest metallic bronze to black; lower chest and abdomen metallic green to brown; tail and wing feather dark; white tufts on sides of tail at base. **FEMALE** Chin and throat white, off-white or gray; head and back dull metallic green, with head darker; white streak and dark patch behind eye.
COMPARISON	Similar in size to blue-throated hummingbird, but magnificent has purple head and green throat; blue-throated has white tips on tail.

TOTAL LENGTH	4.5–5.25" 114–133 mm	**WING LENGTH**	2.75–2.9" 70–76 mm
WEIGHT	.28 oz 8 gm	**TAIL**	long, forked
		BILL LENGTH	1–1.2" 26–31 mm

RANGE	Migratory bird found from April–November in western New Mexico and southeastern Arizona south through central Mexico to Central America. Occasional sightings in western Texas and Colorado.
HABITAT	Open forests of oak or conifers, mixed forest and brushy areas, near streams, low mountain slopes.
FOOD	Penstemons, century plant, agave, honeysuckle, lobelia, Indian bean, insects.
BREEDING	Mating: April–July. Nesting in trees relatively high above ground; nests made of plant fibers and moss, camouflaged with lichen. 2 eggs: incubation unknown. First flight: unknown.
VOCAL CALL	Loud, high-pitched musical "chirp."
HABITS	Mildy territorial. Males and females perch high within their feeding territory.

RANGE OF MAGNIFICENT HUMMINGBIRD

Represents traditional range of species, including some migratory areas. Expansion of range may include more territory within states than is indicated.

● Represents states where species is also occasionally sighted.

Represents normal migratory area outside of breeding territory.

**RUBY-THROATED
HUMMINGBIRD**
FEMALE

**RUBY-THROATED
HUMMINGBIRD**
MALE

VITAL STATISTICS

OFFICIAL NAME	Ruby-throated hummingbird *Archilochus colubris*
COMMON NAMES	Spanish: chupaflor rubi
DESCRIPTION	Small-sized hummingbird. Only hummingbird found in eastern North America. Dark, long, straight bill. Dark, long tail with deep notch when folded. Males smaller than females. Males and females much heavier before migration. **MALE** Chin and throat metallic ruby red; head and back metallic green; small white patch behind eye; chest and abdomen white to off-white; sides tinged with green; tail and wing feathers dark. **FEMALE** Chin and throat white; head and back dull metallic green; small white patch behind eye; chest and abdomen white to gray or buff; white tips on outer tail feathers.
COMPARISON	Similar to broad-tailed hummingbird, but smaller and with forked tail. Similar to Anna's hummingbird, but smaller and without red on head. Similar to black-chinned hummingbird except for color of chin and throat.

TOTAL LENGTH	3–3.75" 76–95 mm	**WING LENGTH**	1.5–1.6" 37–40 mm
WEIGHT	.09–.14 oz 2.5–4 gm	**TAIL**	long, forked
		BILL LENGTH	.59–.67" 15–17 mm

RANGE	Eastern North America from Canada to Gulf of Mexico and Atlantic coast inland to Great Plains (end of Mississippi River region). Migratory from March–October. Winters in central and southern Mexico and Central America, with occasional wintering in Gulf states. Occasional sightings in western states.
HABITAT	Hardwood and conifer forests, meadows, wetlands, hillsides; also common in gardens, parks, and urban areas.
FOOD	Wide variety of flowering plants, shrubs, and trees, especially honeysuckle, trumpet vine, mint.
BREEDING	Mating: spring to early summer. Nesting in trees, usually 5–15 feet above the ground; nests made of scales from plant buds, attached to small branches with spider silk; nests usually sited under overhanging vegetation. 2 eggs: incubation 16 days. First flight: 14–28 days. May have 2 broods.
VOCAL CALL	High-pitched squeak. Single notes or chatter.
HABITS	Very territorial. Males and females defend feeding zones; females also defend nesting area. Males have display flights in wave pattern, also dive in steep "U" during courtship.

RANGE OF RUBY-THROATED HUMMINGBIRD

▨ Represents traditional range of species, including some migratory areas. Expansion of range may include more territory within states than is indicated.

● Represents states where species is also occasionally sighted.

▨ Represents normal migratory area outside of breeding territory.

RUFOUS HUMMINGBIRD
FEMALE

RUFOUS HUMMINGBIRD
MALE

VITAL STATISTICS

OFFICIAL NAME	Rufous hummingbird *Selasphorus rufus*
COMMON NAMES	Spanish: chupamirto dorada
DESCRIPTION	Medium-sized hummingbird. Reddish-brown or rusty (rufous) color. Dark, long, straight bill. Short, pointed tail when folded. Males slightly smaller than females. **MALE** Chin and throat metallic red; head dull metallic bronze-green or bronze; white patch behind eye; white chest; abdomen white to buff; sides buff to rusty; back rusty; tail rusty; wings dark. **FEMALE** Chin and throat white with small patch of metallic red and regular pattern of dark spots; head and back dull metallic green; tail dark with tinge of rust except for green inner feathers; white tips on outside tail feathers.
COMPARISON	Only N.A. hummingbird with rufous color on head and back. Female very similar to Allen's; somewhat similar to broad-tailed except smaller.

TOTAL LENGTH	3.3–3.75" 84–95 mm	**WING LENGTH**	1.5–1.7" 38–42 mm
WEIGHT	.11–.14 oz 3–4 gm	**TAIL**	long, pointed
		BILL LENGTH	.6–.7" 15–18 mm

RANGE	Migratory birds found from February–October from southern Alaska through western Canada, Washington, Oregon, Idaho, Montana south through western states to southern Mexico. Winters throughout Mexico, southern areas of California, Arizona, New Mexico, and Texas. Occasional sightings in eastern states.
HABITAT	Conifer forests, mixed forests, meadows, chaparral; coast to above timberline.
FOOD	Red columbine, currant, salmonberry, manzanita, ocotillo, fireweed, Indian paintbrush, penstemon, agave, figwort, bee plant, madrone, honeysuckle.
BREEDING	Mating: April–June. Nesting in variety of trees and bushes and at different heights; nests made from plant fibers and camouflaged with pieces of bark and lichen. 2 eggs: incubation 15–17 days. First flight: 20–30 days.
VOCAL CALL	Low "chip, chip, chip." Distinctive wing noises when courting, including buzzes and rattles.
HABITS	Territorial. Males and females use high perches to guard territories. Males fly oval pattern during courtship. During hover, tail held high and still.

RANGE OF RUFOUS HUMMINGBIRD

Represents traditional range of species, including some migratory areas. Expansion of range may include more territory within states than is indicated.

● Represents states where species is also occasionally sighted.

Represents normal migratory area outside of breeding territory.

VIOLET-CROWNED
HUMMINGBIRD
FEMALE

VIOLET-CROWNED
HUMMINGBIRD
MALE

VITAL STATISTICS

OFFICIAL NAME	Violet-crowned hummingbird *Amazilia violiceps*
COMMON NAMES	azure-crown hummingbird, Salvin's hummingbird Spanish: chupamirto corona azul
DESCRIPTION	Large-sized hummingbird. Bill is long, curved slightly down, and red or rosy in color except for a dark tip. The tail is slightly forked when folded. Males slightly larger than females. **MALE** Chin, throat, chest, and abdomen are white; head is metallic violet or purple; back is metallic green to bronze-green; tail is olive green to dark green; wings are brown to dark brown. **FEMALE** Color similar to male, but more drab or dull.
COMPARISON	Males and females distinct from other hummingbirds because of red bill, large size, and white throat, chest, and abdomen.

TOTAL LENGTH	3.75–4.5" 95–114 mm	**WING LENGTH**	2.1–2.4" 53–60 mm
WEIGHT	.18–.21 oz 5–6 gm	**TAIL**	long, squared
		BILL LENGTH	.8–.9" 21–24 mm

RANGE	Migratory birds from June–September in southwestern New Mexico and southeastern Arizona, south through central Mexico to northern Central America. Winters in Mexico. Occasional sightings across Arizona, and in California and Texas.
HABITAT	Canyons, arroyos, hillsides, brushy areas, cottonwood and sycamore groves.
FOOD	Agave, century plant, tree tobacco, and penstemons.
BREEDING	Mating: June–July. Nesting in trees and shrubs. Nest made from plant fiber bound with spider webs, camouflaged with lichens. 2 eggs; incubation about 14 days. First flight: 21–22 days.
VOCAL CALL	Sharp metallic notes in chatter pattern.
HABITS	Unknown.

RANGE OF VIOLET-CROWNED HUMMINGBIRD

▨ Represents traditional range of species, including some migratory areas. Expansion of range may include more territory within states than is indicated.

● Represents states where species is also occasionally sighted.

▨ Represents normal migratory area outside of breeding territory.

WHITE-EARED
HUMMINGBIRD
FEMALE

WHITE-EARED
HUMMINGBIRD
MALE

VITAL STATISTICS

OFFICIAL NAME	White-eared hummingbird *Hylocharis leucotis*
COMMON NAMES	Spanish: Chupaflor oreji-blanco
DESCRIPTION	A medium-sized hummingbird with a distinctive white stripe over and behind the eye. Green back and white to gray underparts. Tail long and squared when folded. Bill red to pink in color with black tip. Males slightly larger than females. **MALE** Dark metallic violet to blue on head and on chin next to bill; darker on top of head and below eyes; metallic green throat. Tail has white tips on outer feathers. **FEMALE** Throat and chest spotted with metallic green.
COMPARISON	White eye stripe similar to that of blue-throated, violet-crowned, and broad-billed; red bill similar to violet-crowned and buff-bellied.

TOTAL LENGTH	3.75" 100 mm	**WING LENGTH**	2.1–2.4" 53–60 mm
WEIGHT	.13 oz 3.6 gm	**TAIL**	long, squared
		BILL LENGTH	.6–.75" 15–19 mm

RANGE	Breeding range in North America limited to extreme southeastern Arizona. Occasional sightings in New Mexico, and western Texas. Winter range from mountains of Central America north through central Mexico in the Sierras.
HABITAT	Mountain slopes and canyons. Favors scrub habitat in oak and pine forests near streams.
FOOD	Small flying insects and wide variety of flowers.
BREEDING	Mating: mating flights of males and females involve paired acrobatics; nests typically low to ground and camouflaged with lichens and mosses. 2 eggs: incubation period unknown. First flight: about 25 days. In southern part of range, females may raise 2 broods.
VOCAL CALL	Repeated, soft bell-like "tink, tink, tink."
HABITS	Males found in group assemblies (called leks) in southern part of their range. 6 or 7 males may maintain a common territory for mating and participate in group singing to attract females. Males and females fan and pump their tails while hovering to feed.

RANGE OF WHITE-EARED HUMMINGBIRD

▦ Represents traditional range of species, including some migratory areas. Expansion of range may include more territory within states than is indicated.

● Represents states where species is also occasionally sighted.

▦ Represents normal migratory area outside of breeding territory.

HYBRID HUMMINGBIRDS

"These beatiful creatures will be known on sight ...
The hummers are peculiar to America." — Elliott Coues, 1872

Hummingbird identification is not always simple to begin with, but it becomes more complicated because some species are known to cross-breed, producing hybrids. These hybrids have colors and feather characteristics that come from both species, with some characteristics dominant and others recessive, producing offspring that are a mix of characteristics from both species and thus visibly different from either species. These differences are usually only apparent in adult males.

Hummingbirds, along with ducks, geese, and grouse, are among the few families of birds in North America that frequently produce hybrid chicks. These cross-mating incidents are only likely in habitats where different species of hummingbirds live close together and are probably influenced by the seasonal scarcity of members of one or the other of the species involved. With hummingbirds, some of the hybrids reported by observers may be more common than others, with rarer mixed parentage resulting from birds that stray out of their normal range or accidentally encounter a member of another species at the right time for mating.

HYBRID PAIRS
- Anna's + Black-chinned   • Anna's + Allen's
- Anna's + Calliope   • Costa's + Broad-tailed
- Costa's + Calliope   • Rufous + Calliope
- Black-chinned + Broad-tailed

EVOLUTION

"There is no group of birds so interesting to the ornithologist or to the casual observer as the Humming-Birds, at once the smallest in size, the most gorgeously beautiful in color, and almost the most abundant in species, of any single family of birds."
— S.F. Baird, *A History of North American Birds*, 1874

W here did hummingbirds come from? Unlike many other animals and birds, no fossil evidence has yet been found to indicate what the predecessors of hummingbirds may have been like. Hummingbirds are members of the order *Apodiformes*, which includes swifts. Early forms of this order probably fed exclusively on insects, seeking them out as the insects fed on plant nectar. The bill shape that made this efficient also gave early hummingbirds easy access to the nectar, which gradually became part of their diet.

At the same time, the flowers that were frequented by these birds in their hunting activity became more specialized to take advantage of the frequent visitors and their ability to spread pollen, a critical activity that determines the fate of future flower generations. Such cooperative development between plants and animals is common in the natural world, with some species becoming exclusively dependent on one another. Some modern hummingbird species, in fact, feed primarily on certain kinds of flowers, and these flowers are in turn pollinated exclusively by those hummingbirds.

Despite the lack of fossil evidence, most ornithologists believe that hummingbirds originated in South America, where most of the modern species are now found. Hummingbird species that are found in North America are much less diverse than those found in South America, and the North American species are only seasonal visitors here. The species that migrate north have bills closely matched in length and the species are all relatively small.

SCIENTIFIC CLASSIFICATION

KINGDOM • Animals
PHYLUM • Chordata (vertebrates)
CLASS • Aves (birds)
ORDER • Apodidae (swifts)
FAMILY • Trochilidae (hummingbirds)
GENUS • Stellula
SPECIES • Calliope

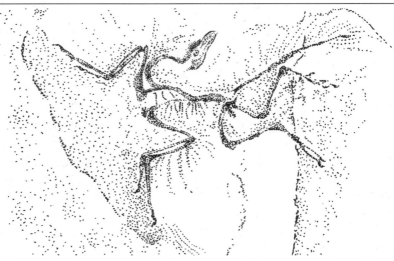

The earliest known fossil of a bird is the *Archaeopteryx*, found in limestone deposits in Germany that date to the Jurassic period, an era that began about 190 million years ago and lasted more than 50 million years. The *Archaeopteryx* was about the size of a crow and is the first fossil found with evidence of feathers.

A VERY UNIQUE BIRD

How are hummingbirds different from other birds?

COLOR — iridescent coloring in some feathers

FEATHERS — no secondary (downy) feathers; least number of feathers of all birds

BRAIN — largest brain in proportion to body size

FLIGHT — fastest wing beat, only bird capable of true hovering and backward flight; only bird with upstroke power equal to downstroke

MUSCLES — breast muscles largest of all birds relative to body size

HEART — largest heart relative to body size (maximum of about 2.4 percent of body weight); most rapid heartbeat of all birds (maximum of 1260 beats per minute)

LUNGS — greatest oxygen consumption (12 times more than the pigeon)

METABOLISM — greatest energy output relative to body size of all warm-blooded animals; only bird that can become torpid

APPETITE — in one day can consume half of its weight in food and eight times its weight in water

EGGS — smallest eggs of all birds

FAMILY SIZE — second largest family of birds in Western hemisphere

WORLD BIRDS

ORDER	DESCRIPTION	No. of SPECIES	No. of FAMILIES
STRUTHIONIFORMES	ostriches	1	1
RHEIFORMES	rheas	2	1
CASUARIIFORMES	cassowaries, emus	4	2
APTERYGIFORMES	kiwis	3	1
TINAMIFORMES	tinamous	45	1
SPHENISCIFORMES	penguins	16	1
GAVIFORMES	loons	4	1
PODICIPEDIFORMES	grebes	20	1
PROCELLARIIFORMES	albatross, petrels	93	4
PELECANIFORMES	pelicans, gannets, cormorants	57	6
CICONIIFORMES	herons, storks, flamingos	115	6
ANSERIFORMES	ducks, geese, swans	150	2
FALCONIFORMES	vultures, eagles, hawks	286	5
GALLIFORMES	grouse, turkeys, quail	256	6
GRUIFORMES	cranes, limpkins, sunbitterns	197	12
CHARADRIIFORMES	auks, snipes, plovers, gulls	319	17
COLUMBIFORMES	pigeons, doves	316	2
PSITTACIFORMES	parrots, macaws, lovebirds	330	1
CUCULIFORMES	turacos, cuckoos, roadrunners	151	3
STRIGIFORMES	owls	134	2
CAPRIMULGIFORMES	oilbirds, nightjars	96	5
APODIFORMES	hummingbirds, swifts	403	3
COLIIFORMES	mousebirds	6	1
TROGONIFORMES	trogons	35	1
CORACIIFORMES	kingfishers, hornbills	193	9
PICIFORMES	toucans, woodpeckers, barbets	376	6
PASSERIFORMES	larks, wrens, dippers, starlings, orioles, crows, tanagers, finches	5219	63

WORLD HUMMINGBIRDS

These are a few of the 320 species of hummingbirds that are found in South America, Central America, and the Caribbean.

BEE

LONG-TAILED
SYLPH

GIANT

SWORD-
BILLED

EASTERN
STREAMERTAIL

ANTILLEAN
CRESTED

ANATOMY

"They are very small, always on the wing, swift as light, of very varied and curious forms, and splendid with gorgeous colors, which flash in the sunlight like the most brilliant and precious gems." — Selim H. Peabody, 1879

One of the reasons that hummingbirds appeal to a wide variety and number of people is their appearance. Hummingbirds are rarely confused with other birds because of their small size, iridescent feathers, needle-like beaks, and unique hovering flight. But telling one species of hummingbird from another is not always simple, except in the eastern half of North America. In this region, the only regular hummingbird resident is the ruby-throated hummingbird, except in Florida and parts of the Gulf coast.

Size variations and distinctive coloration are important defining characteristics for adult male hummingbirds, but no such clear distinctions separate the females or juveniles. In fact, among some hummingbird species, the females may vary more in coloration from one to another than compared with the females of other hummingbird species. At the same time, the females of several species are closely similar in coloration to one another. Another confusing identification factor is among young male hummingbirds. During the growth stage just before they mature into adults, they usually have non-typical coloration patterns that may cause them to look temporarily more like another species than the adults they will soon become. Confusion between hummingbird species is most often found between rufous and Allen's hummingbirds, and between ruby-throated and black-chinned hummingbirds. The best clues for keeping these identities straight include geography, vocal patterns, distinctive coloration details, and behavior.

IDENTIFICATION FEATURES

BILLS The shape, length, width, and color of the bill differs from species to species. Bills on males and females of the same species are usually similar. Bills on juveniles are usually shorter than on adults.

TAILS Tails vary by length, color, and shape. Observation of this feature sometimes requires a view of the tail when spread, but most species do not spread the tail except when hovering.

WINGS Wings vary by length and shape, with minor variations in coloring.

BACKS All North American species have iridescent green coloration on the back, but the color varies from species to species. The edges of feathers on the back may also have distinctive paler tones, usually marking a period just after a molt.

UNDERPARTS Underparts vary by color and the degree of shading, with some iridescent feathers in some species.

IRIDESCENCE Iridescent coloring varies by hue and intensity. Color patterns also vary by species, with iridescent feathers on top and sides of heads, throat (gorget), chest and other underparts, back, and wing covers.

HUMMINGBIRD SKELETON

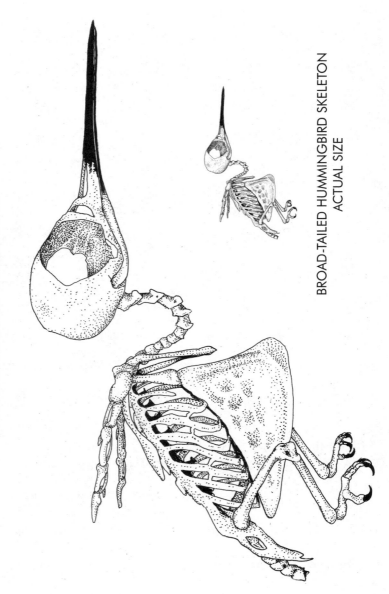

BROAD-TAILED HUMMINGBIRD SKELETON
ACTUAL SIZE

HUMMINGBIRD SKULL
(BROAD-TAILED HUMMINGBIRD)

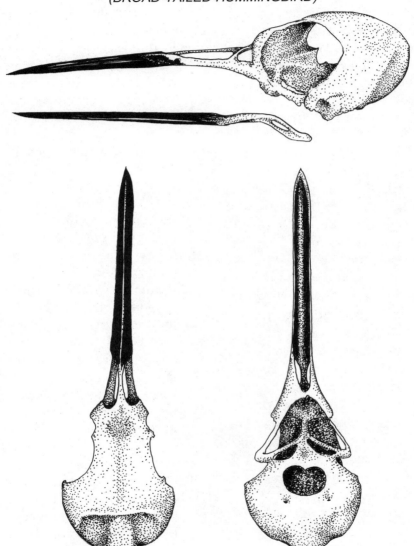

COLOR

One of the primary characteristics of hummingbirds is their unique coloration, at least among the males. Unlike most other birds, however, the colors that make hummingbirds distinctive are not produced by pigments, but created by the reflection of light off unique filmy layers of the barbules of their feathers. Light hitting this layer is reflected or broken down by refraction into iridescent colors that span the complete visible spectrum. The refraction comes from granules of melanin that are formed into oval shapes called platelets, themselves organized into rows. The different colors produced during reflection are determined by the thickness of the platelets and the presence of microscopic air bubbles in them. Depending on the angle of the light, the same bird may appear to be one of several different colors.

Hummingbird feathers have more than one type of reflecting structure. On the throat and crown of the head, the feature structure directs reflected light in a single direction, producing the effect of a color change as the bird flies around the observer. Depending on the angle of sight, the color may appear to change dramatically — from ruby red to green or even to black, for example — in the ruby-

> "On this little bird nature has profusely lavished her most splendid colors ...The richest pallet of the most luxuriant painter, could never invent any thing to be compared to the variegated tints, with which this insect bird is arrayed ... Its little eyes appear like diamonds, reflecting light on every side: most elegantly finished in all parts it is a miniature work of our great parent; who seems to have formed it the smallest, and at the same time the most beautiful of the winged species."
> — Hector St. John de Crèvecoeur

throated hummingbird. On the birds' backs, however, the feather structure diffuses the reflection of light, scattering it in multiple directions and providing to an observer the appearance of a single hue — usually green — no matter what the angle of viewing.

All hummingbird feathers also have pigment, however, creating an additional source of colors. The iridescent, metallic colors of the throat, crown, and back include green, red, blue, and violet produced by refraction. Only two types of pigments, however, are found in the feathers, limiting the colors produced by this source to a variety of browns, reddish browns, and black. The iridescent feathers have pigments in the lower half, mostly hidden by the overlap of other iridescent feathers.

A single feather consists of many individual barbules — strands of tissue that are made up of smaller interlocking fibers.

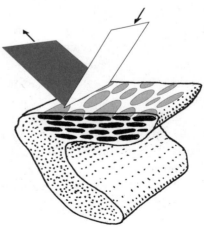

Inside the structure of the barbule strands are microscopic particles called platelets, which refract incoming light into separate colors.

FEET

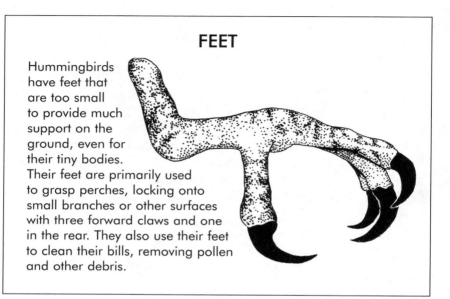

Hummingbirds have feet that are too small to provide much support on the ground, even for their tiny bodies. Their feet are primarily used to grasp perches, locking onto small branches or other surfaces with three forward claws and one in the rear. They also use their feet to clean their bills, removing pollen and other debris.

FEATHERS

Feathers cover the entire hummingbird body, with the exception of the bill, eyes, and feet. There are only about 1,000 to 1,500 feathers on a single hummingbird, the smallest number among all birds. Some larger birds have many more feathers; a swan can have more than 25,000 feathers, not counting its down. But still, compared to the surface area of its tiny body, the hummingbird may have one of the densest sets of feathers of all bird groups, that is, the most feathers compared to its body size. Also, compared to its weight, the hummingbird has a heavier proportion of feathers than other birds. While the swan has 112 feathers per ounce of body weight (4 feathers per gram), the hummingbird carries 84 times as many, or 9,380 per ounce (although, of course, hummingbirds weigh less than an ounce).

The outer, visible set of plumage on birds is made up of contour feathers. An inner, secondary set of feathers is called down, smaller and fluffier than contour feathers, and providing an efficient layer of insulation next to the body. Down, however, is not found on any of the hummingbird species, one of many ways they differ from other birds. The lack of down may be an asset because it saves weight and bulk, but it also restricts the ability of hummingbirds to conserve heat and is one of the reasons they have developed the ability to enter a state called torpidity. Hummingbird chicks are sometimes born with down, or develop some within a few days after hatching, but it is sparse and falls out by the time the birds grow their adult feathers.

The wing feathers of the hummingbird are among its most unique feathers compared to other birds. The primary feathers, for instance, are largest on the outermost section of the wing while all

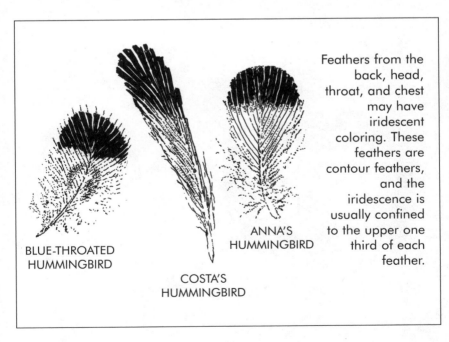

BLUE-THROATED
HUMMINGBIRD

COSTA'S
HUMMINGBIRD

ANNA'S
HUMMINGBIRD

Feathers from the back, head, throat, and chest may have iridescent coloring. These feathers are contour feathers, and the iridescence is usually confined to the upper one third of each feather.

other birds have their largest primary feathers on the innermost wing section. The size of the hummingbird's primary feathers gets progressively smaller from the outside to the inside. The tail and wing feathers have little, if any, iridescent coloring.

The feathers on the throat, or gorget, of the hummingbird are the most distinctive on its body, providing the brightest iridescent colors. These feathers overlap like shingles with only the lower one third being iridescent. This section of the iridescent feathers is the only one visible.

BILLS

Hummingbird bills come in a wide assortment of sizes and shapes, but each is well-suited to connect the bird to its major food source, nectar. The bill design allows it access to the inner portions of flowers, where the nectar is found. Although all hummingbird bills are long and narrow to accomplish the task of getting to flower nectar, there is variation in length, width, shape, and color of bills among various hummingbird species.

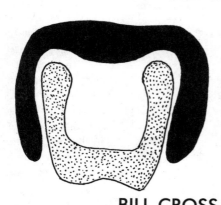

The hummingbird is the only bird with an overlapping bill. The top bill fits over and around the lower bill.

BILL CROSS-SECTION

In North America, hummingbird species have a broader range of habitats and the food supplies of different species often overlap. Correspondingly, the variety of bill shapes found in the North American species is not as extreme as those in the southern species because the birds must feed from a wider variety of flower structures. All of the hummingbirds found here have bills that are either straight or curved slightly down, but all are relatively long, at least the length of the bird's head but in a few cases almost twice this measurement. Males and females of most hummingbird species are often close to each other in size — in some species, males are slightly larger than females, in others the ratio is reversed or there is no difference — but female bills are almost always longer than males for birds of the same species.

Unlike most other birds, hummingbird bills have a pronounced overlap, with the upper bill curving around and over the sides of the smaller lower bill. When hummingbirds feed, the bill is usually only opened slightly, allowing the bill-shaped tongue to dart out and into the interior of flowers. The bill is rarely opened wide — and in any case is limited in how far it can be opened — but is used for a variety of tasks, including catching insects in flight, preening feathers, carrying nesting material, constructing nests, feeding baby hummingbirds, and attacking rivals.

Bill shapes among North American species vary mostly by the degree of curvature. Most of these hummingbird types have straight, or mostly straight, bills but the Lucifer hummingbird has a bill that curves downward in a shallow arc. In comparison, the mountain avocetbill hummingbird in South America has a bill that curves upward, and the white-tipped sicklebill hummingbird, also found in South America, curves downward in an extreme arc. Bills have a sharp point at the end and are uniformly narrow from tip to base. But a few species feature bills that are noticeably wider, like the broad-billed hummingbird, or wider at the base, like the violet-crowned and the buff-bellied hummingbirds.

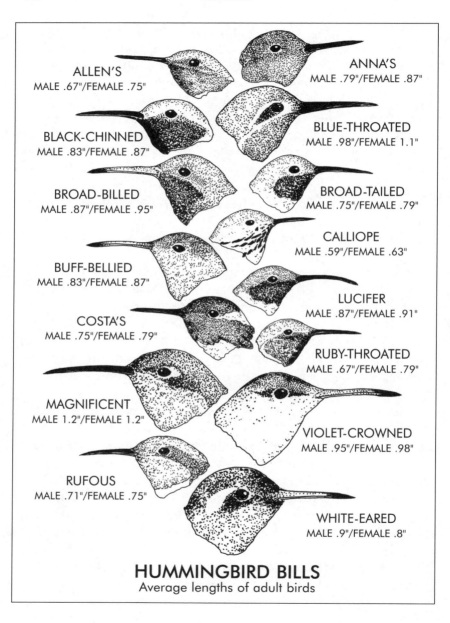

ALLEN'S
MALE .67"/FEMALE .75"

ANNA'S
MALE .79"/FEMALE .87"

BLACK-CHINNED
MALE .83"/FEMALE .87"

BLUE-THROATED
MALE .98"/FEMALE 1.1"

BROAD-BILLED
MALE .87"/FEMALE .95"

BROAD-TAILED
MALE .75"/FEMALE .79"

BUFF-BELLIED
MALE .83"/FEMALE .87"

CALLIOPE
MALE .59"/FEMALE .63"

COSTA'S
MALE .75"/FEMALE .79"

LUCIFER
MALE .87"/FEMALE .91"

RUBY-THROATED
MALE .67"/FEMALE .79"

MAGNIFICENT
MALE 1.2"/FEMALE 1.2"

VIOLET-CROWNED
MALE .95"/FEMALE .98"

RUFOUS
MALE .71"/FEMALE .75"

WHITE-EARED
MALE .9"/FEMALE .8"

HUMMINGBIRD BILLS
Average lengths of adult birds

Although male hummingbirds typically feature the brightest colors and are often larger than females, the bills of females are usually slightly longer than those of males of the same species. The longest bill found among North American species is about 1-1/4", found on the magnificent hummingbird; the shortest is about 1/2", found on the calliope hummingbird. In comparison, the longest bill among all hummingbirds is found on the sword-billed hummingbird in South America, a beak that can grow to four inches in length. The shortest hummingbird beak is found on the bee hummingbird, about 1/4" in length.

Most hummingbirds have bills that are dark in color, and in most cases almost black. A few species, however, sport distinctively colorful bills. The broad-billed, buff-bellied, and violet-crowned hummingbirds have bills that are reddish, rosy, or coral in color. These species usually have a darker color at the tip of the bill, and the bills of females and juveniles of the same species may have less of the same color.

TONGUES

While the hummingbird bill is designed for easy access to flowers, the tongue contained within the bill is designed for efficient extraction of the nectar that flowers contain. Fitting neatly inside the bill, it is a long, narrow organ consisting of flesh and cartilage. In color, it is pale, almost white, and translucent. At the base, the tongue is wider and flatter and a single tubular unit. Near the midpoint in length, the tongue divides into two tube-like structures, each with a thin strip of cartilage along the edge. This strip is divided into tiny, irregular fringes toward the tip of the tongue, an adaptation that may aid the bird in gathering nectar and insects. In construction, each lobe of the tongue is much like a tube created by rolling up a flat membrane, but is not hollow like a straw. The tongue in action is usually moving too fast for observers to see.

The exact process in which a hummingbird tongue extracts liquid nectar from a flower is not clearly understood, but it is thought to involve a combination of actions. Some of the liquid is captured in droplets by the fringed strip on the edges of the two tongue parts and some is drawn into the fringes by capillary action. When the tongue is pulled back into the bill, the nectar is sucked and scraped off of and out of the tongue, readying it for another trip outside. In action, the tongue flicks in and out very fast, from 10 to 15 times per second. Insects are also pulled into the mouth by the tongue in the same way.

> "The tongue is the chief weapon for capturing their prey and sucking up their nectar, and consists of a long double tube, formed like a double-barreled gun; at the tip it is flattened, and sometimes barbed. It is darted out with great dexterity, and is thus a very efficient instrument."
> — THE ANIMAL KINGDOM, 1867

Hummingbird tongues and other soft tissue in their mouths contain taste buds that are critical tools in choosing food sources. They can differentiate between liquids based on the amount of sugar content and can usually select nectar — or sugar solutions in feeders — that is the sweetest. But hummingbirds, like all birds, only have about 50 taste buds — 1 percent of the number found in human tongues — and are unlikely to make more complex choices about food based on its taste.

North American hummingbirds are capable of extending their tongues about the same length as their bills. In some species of flowers, this extreme extension may be necessary to reach the stored

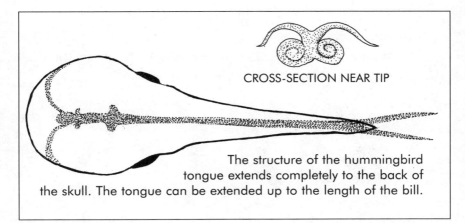

CROSS-SECTION NEAR TIP

The structure of the hummingbird
tongue extends completely to the back of
the skull. The tongue can be extended up to the length of the bill.

nectar. In one study of hummingbird feeding behavior, the longer
the flower tubes, the more time required for the hummingbirds to
extract the nectar. This is because the tongue, when it is traveling
a longer distance, takes more time to do its work. The narrowness
of flower tubes also has an impact on how far the tongue can be
extended; in some flower species, hummingbirds are unable to
remove all of the nectar that is available.

TAILS

Variations in hummingbird tails include those that are forked or square and those that are longer in the middle or longer on the outside. Tail feathers also vary in shape, length, and color.

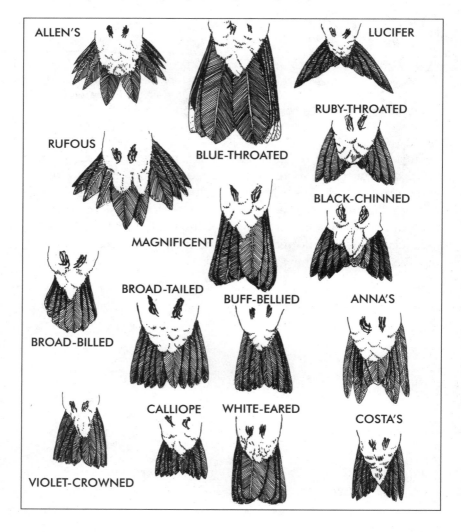

MOLTING

"In those warm climates, where the Bigonias and other tubular flowers that bloom throughout the year, and innumerable insects that sport in the sun-shine, afford an abundance of food, these lively birds are the greatest ornaments of the gardens and forests. Such in most cases is the brilliancy of their plumage, that I am unable to find apt objects of comparison unless I resort to the most brilliant gems and the richest metals."

— Reverend John Bachman, 1840

Birds experience a periodic growth of new feathers and shedding of their old feathers, a condition called molting, similar to the shedding of fur in mammals. Molting begins before birds have reached maturity, allowing the feathers that baby birds develop soon after being born to be replaced with stronger, larger feathers that are better suited for flying. Hummingbird babies develop their first coat of feathers in two to three weeks.

For hummingbirds, the first molt typically occurs about one year after hatching. Until that time, both male and female birds resemble each other; after the first molt, the males of most species acquire a more distinctive plumage than the females, primarily different on the head and throat. During a molt, each new feather that grows in may take several weeks to attain its full size and shape. But if a bird loses one or more feathers in a non-molting period — feathers damaged during an accident or a fight with another bird, for example — replacement feathers may appear and mature in less time. Altogether, it may take up to four months for all of the feathers on a hummingbird to be replaced, because the feathers — at least on the tail and wings — generally get replaced one at a time. Although one bird may go through a molting cycle in about four months, hummingbirds of a single species do not molt together. The staggered molting schedule among all the birds in the same species may last up to eight months.

As the contour feathers are used in flight, they gradually wear away and become less efficient. Regular molting is a necessary function because feathers, like hair on mammals, are dead tissue and cannot regrow worn or damaged surfaces. A new feather grows out from the follicle at its base, gradually pushing out the old feather. The exchange process for all the feathers does not happen at a single moment, but occurs in patterns over a bird's body. The timing of the pattern allows hummingbirds, in most cases, to continue flying and feeding, although they do so at a slower pace than when not molting.

The first feathers to molt are the primary feathers on the wings, beginning with the first, or innermost feather, with symmetrical molting on both sides of the body. About the time that the new wing feathers have emerged and reached full size, the tail feathers begin their molt. After wing and tail, feathers on the other parts of the body begin their molt, including the plumage on the back and underparts. Often, the last new feathers to appear are on the most spectacular zones of the body, the gorget (chin and throat), and the head. Because most species molt before the beginning of the breeding season, this gives the males a new and attractive set of plumage just when it is most useful — for courtship and defense of territory. And because the breeding season for North American species usually follows close behind the migration up from the south, a molt also provides strong, undamaged feathers for this flight.

On the flight south during late summer and fall months, however, hummingbirds must get by with worn-out plumage. Most bird watchers in North America miss seeing molting in action because it happens during the winter period when most North American hummingbird species are in Mexico and Central America. These species typically begin their molts from September to November, just after they arrive on the southward leg of their migration cycle.

As a new feather emerges, it is called a pinfeather and is visibly different from the feather it replaces. The pinfeather is a white or light-colored shaft resembling the quill of a porcupine. This appearance comes from the nature of the new feather, which has been created with the top part folded tightly into itself and held in place by a thin membrane wrapped around the outer surface. Shortly after the pinfeather has first emerged, the membrane splits apart, allowing the top barbules of the feather to spread out; the main shaft of the feather emerges underneath this portion.

ALBINO HUMMINGBIRDS

Although very rare, hummingbirds are sometimes born with no pigment in their feathers. Just as in mammals that have this condition, these birds also have pink eyes because of missing pigment. Some of these hummingbirds may be partial albinos, with splotches or streaks of gray or brown in some of their feathers. Most feathers will still have some iridescent qualities because this metallic reflection is created by other structures in the feathers other than pigment. In albino hummingbirds, however, the reflective colors will be different than in members of the species with normal pigmentation because some of the normal metallic color is influenced by pigments in the noniridescent layers of the feathers.

BODY TEMPERATURE

"Whoever watches a female busy about her nest will see her constantly perching here and there in certain branches of the tree, preening her plumage and looking about her. The male, at the same season, forgetful, to all appearance, of his conjugal and parental duties, may be found at home day after day on a dead twig in some tall tree, where he sits so constantly as to make the observer wonder what he can be about, and when, if ever, he takes his food."
— Frank M. Chapman, 1932

Hummingbirds are the smallest birds on the planet. Like all animals, body temperature is primarily linked to their size, in particular the ratio of surface area to body volume. As with all small animals, this ratio is very high, meaning more of the body mass is directly exposed to the outside world than animals of a larger size. For other animals, large bodies are compensated by relatively less surface exposure and therefore less space in which their bodies may be gaining or losing heat from the environment. Hummingbirds must spend proportionately more energy just to maintain their body temperature than larger animals just because of their size. And their problem is compounded because, of their total body mass, about 30 percent is muscle tissue — the power source for their unique flying capabilities — and these muscles burn energy at a rapid rate.

In their daily lives, this means a large part of their time is spent gathering and consuming food, the resource from which they generate body heat. Their bodies carry little capacity for storing energy in the form of fat; food is turned into energy almost as fast as it is consumed. At night, tiny animals such as these are at a serious disadvantage because they are resting instead of feeding. If the outside temperature drops below a certain level, hummingbirds would die without a special adaptation. Nature's solution for the humming-bird is a special resting state called torpor (also called noctivation, a term credited to Alexander Skutch).

During this state, hummingbird body temperatures drop dramatically from their normal daytime highs, sometimes sinking almost to the temperature of the surrounding air. Resting hummingbirds have been found with body temperatures as low as 70 degrees F. Sleeping hummingbirds which are not in a state of torpor typically experience a drop of only 4–8 degrees F. in body temperature. The result of torpor is a drastic reduction in energy consumption by the bird's body. Hummingbirds in this state may use as little as one-sixtieth of the energy their bodies would require when at normal temperature. While experiencing this torpidity, their breathing may be irregular and could, in some extreme states of cold, stop altogether for long periods of time. At the same time, hummingbird hearts may slow to about 150 beats per minute, compared to normal waking heart rates of more than 1,000 beats per minute.

Hummingbirds do not enter a state of torpor every night, nor do all species in all climates exhibit this behavior. Whether or not a hummingbird enters this state may be influenced by its diet, its health, and the type of seasonal behavior it is experiencing, such as mating. Female hummingbirds that are incubating eggs, for example, do not experience torpor because a higher body temperature is required to keep the eggs warm. Even after the eggs have hatched, the mother hummingbird must maintain a normal body temperature, or the young birds can suffer physical harm and experience arrested development.

Some hummingbird species in South America live in climates where the nighttime temperature drops below freezing. In these areas, hummingbirds typically seek out protected spots in which to spend the night, usually with other hummingbirds or even other bird species. With these hummingbirds, the period of torpor is also different, in that the birds' internal temperature does not continu-

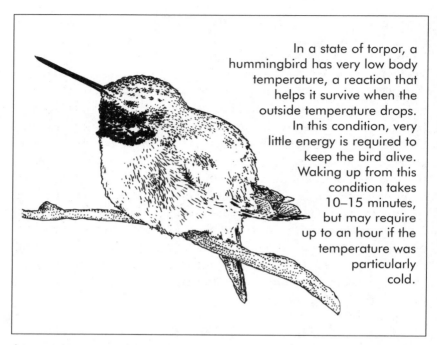

In a state of torpor, a hummingbird has very low body temperature, a reaction that helps it survive when the outside temperature drops. In this condition, very little energy is required to keep the bird alive. Waking up from this condition takes 10–15 minutes, but may require up to an hour if the temperature was particularly cold.

ously drop along with the outside temperature. At some point — in one area of the Andes where it was measured, the point was around 41 degrees F. — a new condition is triggered, called thermoregulation. When this happens, the birds' metabolisms begin to generate a small amount of heat, enough to remain at a stable level.

To get from a resting state, or torpor — during which a bird is more or less in a trance — to normal, daylight activity, a hummingbird uses a "fast start" method of recovering its senses. As the sun rises, energy reserves in the body are used to generate a rapid, energetic shivering, increasing the heartbeat and body temperature. In ten or fifteen minutes, most hummingbirds have returned to a normal, waking state, with an internal temperature of about 86 degrees F., thought to be the minimum required for flight. Some North American hummingbird species are also thought to have an internal clock that triggers this action before the sun rises or there is a rise in the temperature of the air. In colder climates, such as the South American Andes, hummingbirds may take an hour or more to reverse the state of torpor.

When sleeping, hummingbirds perch differently than most other birds. Their heads, instead of being tucked under wings or into shoulders, pose straight forward and tilted slightly back. In this position, their bills point up. To help conserve heat, their feathers are fluffed out during this period of rest.

Low temperatures are not the only negative effect on hummingbirds from the environment. During hot days they may also be harmed by high temperatures. Because birds do not moderate their body temperature through the skin (they lack sweat glands that perform this function in mammals) and worse, their feathers trap heat from radiating away from their skin, they use another method of cooling down — panting rapidly through open bills.

WASTES

Hummingbirds, although small, have digestive systems that work much like those of other birds, including the generation of waste. Urine and feces leave the body through the vent, usually combined together into droppings.

THE HUMMINGBIRD DIET

"The Hummingbird is curiously fearless. Sometimes one will probe a flower held in the hand, and when they fly into houses, as they pretty often do, they manifest but the smallest degree of suspicion, and will feed almost at once upon sugar held between the lips."

— Bradford Torrey, 1932

Hummingbirds are popularly thought to live only on the nectar of plants. The widespread use of hummingbird feeders — dispensing sugar water as an ersatz nectar — helps support this notion, but it is not true. Hummingbirds in North America seek out and eat the nectar of many types of flowers, as well as tree sap and other sources of natural sugar, but they also consume large quantities of insects.

Hummingbirds frequently hunt insects on the fly, catching them in the air. They may also hover around flowers to capture the insects that are also attracted to the blossoms for their nectar. Some observers have seen hummingbirds raiding spiders' webs, plucking off captured insects. And some hummingbirds readily target the spiders themselves, as well as the webbing filaments, which are used by female hummingbirds to construct nests. Most often, however, hummingbirds ingest insects that are in or near the nectar the birds seek, capturing these tiny animals with their tongues along with the liquid.

In one experiment with a captive hummingbird, more than 600 fruit flies were eaten by the bird in a single day. The flies were provided along with a supply of sweetened water, which the bird also drank. In one day, the consumption of these insects added up to about 27 percent of the birds weight, with the liquid food providing 73 percent of its weight. In the wild, daily diets of insects may vary considerably from this figure. Insects are primarily a source of protein. Protein in larger amounts can come from their liquid diet, but nectar is most important as a source of carbohydrates.

The minimum dietary requirement of hummingbirds is closely related to their expenditure of energy. Calorie needs may range from 6,000 to more than 12,000 per day, with the amount related to the size of the hummingbird and the activity of the individual bird. Activity itself ranges from typical daylight flights to protect territory and feed, nighttime rest periods that may include torpor, and feeding binges when hummingbirds, such as the ruby-throated species, store up extra energy for migration flights. Females developing eggs and adults of both sexes going through molting periods also require nontypical energy needs.

Analysis of the rufous hummingbird metabolism also indicates that hummingbirds may have the ability to use more than one source of fuel when flying, either burning carbohydrates almost directly as they consume nectar, or switching to stored fat. Fat storage, in turn, may be induced if feeding flights are kept short and other energy-demanding activities — including the defense of its territory — are kept to a minimum. Some biologists believe that this behavior may be used by the ruby-throated hummingbird just before its long migratory flights across the Gulf of Mexico.

The hummingbird may eat almost its own weight in food in a single day, the requirements of a tiny body that needs a lot of energy to maintain its temperature and power its wings for flight. Hummingbirds do not have the ability to store much of the food they digest as fat, one of the reasons it must be ingested frequently and digested quickly. Both nectar and insects are digested rapidly.

In order to extract the maximum energy value from its food, a hummingbird must digest what it eats very efficiently as well as rapidly. Nectar, which is liquid and high in carbohydrates, may be completely digested in less than one hour, according to some studies. While the nectar is passing through the digestive system, about 97 percent of the natural sugars it contains are extracted.

Hummingbirds forage for food most of the daylight hours, but they also often take rests. Periods of time when these birds appear to be resting, however, are actually when they are emptying internal storage areas, making room for more food. Like all birds, hummingbirds have crops, small sacs located at the base of their throats where incoming food is temporarily cached. When sitting on a branch, a hummingbird is quietly transferring nectar or other food from its crop into the active part of its digestive system. Typically, a hummingbird will remove about half the food stored in its crop before flying off to gather more, a cycle that it usually repeats about fifteen times per hour.

When hummingbirds are feeding primarily on nectar, they must consume enough liquid to provide the minimum amount of sugar necessary for their survival. In quantity, this may mean sipping an amount of liquid equivalent to more than 80 percent of the natural water content in their bodies. As the sugar is extracted during digestion, the fluid remaining from the nectar, mostly water, is passed out as urine. An adult human would need to urinate about twenty gallons in a single day to equal this feat. Depending on the nature of the nectar they drink, hummingbird diets may also require additional intake of water.

One exception to the limited ability of the hummingbird to store energy is when it is migrating. Before taking these journeys — some species cross the Gulf of Mexico in a single flight leg of more than 500 miles — the birds build up their resources with an increase in their feeding. Weight gain and loss during a migratory period may be up to 60 percent of the total body weight of the animal, the extreme weight fluctuation among vertebrates. For a human weighing 150 pounds, this would be the equivalent of ballooning to 240 pounds, a gain of 90 pounds. Gray wolves, among the champion gorgers in the mammal class, gain a maximum of 20 percent of their body weight during a feasting session.

How much time a hummingbird must spend feeding depends on

the availability of nectar and insects as well as the calorie content of the nectar. Just as with processed human food, nectar may vary in the amount of usable sugar it contains. Seasonal activities such as mating and the need to defend its territory also affect the time available for feeding. In various studies of different hummingbird species, it has been determined that from 500 to 1,000 blossoms might be required to provide the minimum daily food requirements for a single hummingbird.

When feeding from flowers, hummingbirds usually hover. Because hovering requires the greatest amount of energy expenditure of all the activity they do, feeding must be quick, efficient, and they must rely on flowers with the highest amounts of nectar. When more than one variety of flower is available, hummingbirds will usu-

Hummingbirds can hover in a variety of postures in order to feed from different kinds of flowers.

ally pick the ones that have the highest sugar content and the most nectar.

Not all feeding is done while hovering. Hummingbirds will take advantage of branches, twigs, or leaves to perch while feeding if it is convenient. This action saves them considerable energy, but may also make them more vulnerable to attack by predators.

Like all birds, hummingbirds use their crops to hold food for later digestion. Crops are larger in baby hummingbirds, possibly because at that stage of their lives they are fed larger amounts of insects, which require longer periods of digestion than nectar. But crops can hold both insects and nectar, allowing a bird to stock up with extra food supplies before resting.

Another hummingbird adaptation for digestion that is different from most other birds is its stomach, or gizzard. The entrance and exit of this organ are very close together, allowing fluids to flow through rapidly. When the stomach is full of insects, this permits the most efficient processing of nectar, which is digested farther down in the system, while the stomach proceeds on a slower pace with its own load.

One assessment of the food requirements of a male Anna's hummingbird in a typical 24-hour period determined it required about 7.5 to 12.5 calories to stay alive. During normal activity, this bird would expend 3.8 calories while perching; 2.5 calories flying in nectar gathering activity; 0.1 calories in insect gathering activity; and 0.3 calories defending territory. To acquire these calories, the hummingbird would have to gather the nectar from about 1,000 fuchsia flowers. This calorie intake, however, must be increased if the bird does not enter a state of torpor during sleep, an action that conserves a great deal of energy. Without torpor, one study has determined that an additional 4 calories of food is required from a day's foraging.

Hummingbirds may also feed at different rates at different times of the day. Needing additional stored energy for the prolonged rest period during nighttime hours, some feed most heavily at the end of the day. Other hummingbirds may feed more slowly as the day progresses, possibly because they become heavier and slower from the food they have so far consumed. Feeding on average happens from 5 to 8 times per hour. Between feeding flights, they rest.

FREQUENT FLYERS

Hummingbirds are critical to the survival of at least one animal. Flower mites, tiny arachnids that live their entire life cycles within flowers, must be able to get to new flowers when their current home dies. One species of these arachnids, hummingbird flower mites, accomplish this feat by hitchhiking with hummingbirds as they feed on nectar. When a hummingbird first begins feeding at a flower populated by these animals, some of them quickly crawl onto the bird's bill and enter its nostrils. When the bird flies off and stops at another blossom of the same type, the mites rapidly "deplane" to inhabit a new home. In North America, only one species of this mite has been discovered, *Rhinoseius epoecus*, although dozens of others have been identified in South America. Allen's, Anna's, and rufous hummingbirds are the only birds known to serve the mite as transportation.

FOOD SOURCES

"Although flying from flower to flower in search of food, its stomach generally contained abundant remains of insects, which I suspect are much more the object of its search than honey. The note of this species, like that of nearly the whole family, is extremely shrill."

— Charles Darwin, 1887

Hummingbirds in North America may have few or many types of flowers upon which to feed, depending on the geographic zone in which they live. In California, for example, there are an estimated eighty different species of flowers on the hummingbird menu; in Idaho, there are only fourteen. This has been determined by research carried out by Karen and Verne Grant (published in *Hummingbirds and Their Flowers*).

Plants frequented by hummingbirds are found in a variety of ecosystems, from mountain to desert. At different times of a year — often during migratory movements — hummingbirds may be residents of different zones. Not by accident, flowers in different zones will bloom at different times, but always when hummingbirds are present. Conversely, hummingbirds will only be present if there are appropriate flowers blooming, otherwise they would not be able to survive. Hummingbirds, however, sometimes visit ecological zones when there are few or none of their primary sources of flowering plants. During these periods, they will take advantage of other types of flowers and switch to a higher percentage of insects for nutrition.

Some parts of North America do not support the plant life needed for hummingbird survival. Hummingbirds are not found in alpine habitats above 9,000 feet in mountain areas, in the Mojave Desert, or in grasslands and the central part of some dense forests. The ruby-throated hummingbird is found throughout the eastern United States, for example, with the exception of shoreline habitats and marshes. The other species — all native to western North

America — do not live in most of the Great Plains, where grassland vegetation does not include the flowering plants that traditionally provide them with their major source of food. Also, some of the migratory hummingbirds found in the West travel through non-supportive areas on their way to and from breeding habitats. Their migrations are timed to take advantage of the blooms temporarily found along the way.

Hummingbirds in North America are adaptable animals. Anyone who has put out a hummingbird feeder will attest to how quickly these birds discover and exploit a new source of food. But most hummingbird food sources have been long established. Among the plant life native to this continent, about 150 plants have been determined to have special characteristics that evolved specifically to take advantage of hummingbird feeding.

Flowers on such plants are generally different from those on plants that are not used as primary food sources by hummingbirds. The characteristics that matter most include:

- daytime blooming
- large quantities of nectar
- flowers in red or yellow hues
- nectar collection at the base of long, narrow tubes protected by relatively strong tissue
- flowers with little or no scent
- a lack of structural elements that could be used as perches or landing platforms

With these characteristics, the nectar in the flowers is more likely to be available to hummingbirds and not insects such as bees or butterflies. Also, a general characteristic among many hummingbird plants is a tendency to have longer blooming seasons than other plants. Unlike the case in Central and South America, however, no hummingbird plants in North America have developed to exclusively attract a single hummingbird species. In eastern North America, there is only a single species, but the plants that the ruby-

HUMMINGBIRD ANIMAL MENU

Hummingbirds will eat a variety of small insects and arachnids,
including flies, mosquitoes, aphids, leaf-hoppers, ants and spiders.

throated hummingbird feeds on are thought to be acceptable feeding sources for the other North American species, even if they were
more widely dispersed.

In western North America, hummingbird plants are most often
perennial herbs and softwood plants. Although the blossoms of a
few types of trees are on the hummingbird menu, most of their foraging is done among other plant forms. Because of widespread agri-
culture and gardening activities, nonnative plants may be major
sources of food.

At least one flower in North America has no nutrition to offer
hummingbirds. The cardinal flower — common in the mountains
of Arizona — has no nectar, but its design closely resembles other
local flowers that are major food supplies for hummingbirds.
Hummingbirds that are lured to this plant by its familiarity get
nothing for their efforts, but the plant gains a free ride for its pollen.

Hummingbirds forage for food in several distinctive ways. Some
species stay close to a single flowering plant; these plants usually
feature a large number of blooms and can provide food for more
than one flight or day. This type of feeding is linked most closely to
territoriality, with birds staking out zones to defend. Other species

NORTH AMERICAN HUMMINGBIRD NECTAR MENU

agave
allionia coccinea
aloe
azalea
beard tongue
bee balm
bouvardia
bottlebrush
buckeye
catchfly
century plant
clover
columbine
coral tree
currant
desert honeysuckle (chuparosa)
desert trumpet (skyrocket)
figwort
firecracker plant
fireweed
foxglove
four-o'clocks
fuchsia
gilia
gooseberry
hedge nettle
hedgehog cactus
hollyhock
honeysuckle
Indian paintbrush
Indian pink
jacobinia
jewelweed
ladies tresses
lantana
larkspur

lilac
lily
lobelia
locoweed
lousewort
maguey
manzanita
milkweed
mimosa
mint
monkey flower
morning glory
mountain pennyroyal
ocotillo
palo verde
penstemons
pinkroot
polemonium
red buckeye
red yucca
sage
salmonberry
salvia
scarlet fritillary
scarlet gilia
scarlet lobellia (cardinal flower)
shrimp plant
spotted touch-me-not
star glory
thistles
trumpet vine
twinberry
viburnum
wild bergamont
wooly blue-curls

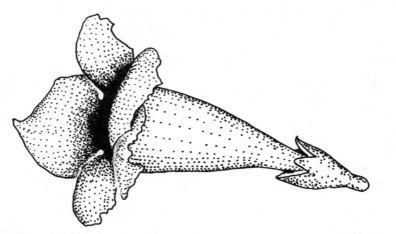

This trumpet vine flower has adapted to be an ideal source of nectar for hummingbirds. It has no scent to attract insects, no perching surfaces for insects, and is red in color, a strong visual signal to hummingbirds.

regularly follow feeding routes, following an aerial path from one plant to another. This behavior is called "traplining," after the traditional method of setting animal traps along a linear route. In North America, neither type of behavior is followed in the extreme because there is generally enough variety of food sources, and not an excessive amount of competition among hummingbird species for it.

In South America, on the other hand, feeding behavior can be more complex. Biologists have found four types of such behavior. These include: high-reward traplining, with species depending on specialized flowers spread over a wide territory; low-reward traplining, with species feeding over a wide territory but depending on a wider variety of flowers; territorialism, species defending distinct areas and feeding off all flowers within that zone; and territory parasitism, with species ignoring territorial defense or sneaking around defenders.

Food preferences influence hummingbird feeding behavior. Although many people believe that they are attracted to a food source only by its color — preferably red — research has determined that hummingbirds are not born with this attraction, but learn it from experience because most of the flowers that produce the nectar they prefer are red in color. Among a variety of flowers, they sample and select those varieties that have the most nectar and the highest concentrations of sugar.

Nectar consists of more than one kind of natural sugar and usually includes combinations of sucrose, glucose, and fructose. In research tests, hummingbirds seem to prefer sucrose the most, and fructose the least, but they will consume any of these when they are available. In North America, almost all of the flowers that are frequent sources of nectar for hummingbirds are highest in sucrose content. Scientists have not been able to figure out why this taste preference exists, because all of these sugars taste similar and all are digested the same way, producing about the same amount of energy in the same amount of time. Flowers may have evolved different sugar contents to attract different kinds of pollinators, but they do not seem to gain any advantage with hummingbirds.

This sugar content occurs in concentrations from a few percent to 80 percent. The higher the sugar content, the more viscous or thick the nectar.

The cardinal flower attracts hummingbirds in order to pollinate, but it has no nectar.

Although the highest concentrations might be more nutritious for the hummingbird, it is stickier and less fluid the higher the concentration of sugar, making it harder to extract with the tongue. In the wild, hummingbirds usually select nectar that has a sugar content of 20–50 percent. Another factor in the quality of the nectar produced by the flower is how much time a hummingbird will need to extract it; the less nectar, the less time spent at the flower, and therefore the less chance of the flower being successfully pollinated. A balance between the attraction and the reward produces flowers that generally have nectar with sugar content of about 25 percent. Many flowers also produce a continuous output of nectar while they are blooming, giving the hummingbird an opportunity to visit on a regular basis.

In some circumstances, the normal hummingbird diet may be unbalanced because of the type of nutrients taken in, the quantity of water absorbed by their body, and the stress of activity they may be undertaking. When building nests, for example, some female hummingbirds have been observed ingesting ashes from wood fires. One conclusion made from this observation is that these birds required additional calcium and minerals in their diet to help them during the production of eggs.

Hummingbirds also seem to have a great capacity for learning about their food sources. In the first place, because they are not born with the ability to know that most of the flowers that are good sources of food are red, they quickly learn by trial and error to select flowers by color. But they also adjust their preferences daily to select food sources, and tests have shown they retain a good memory of flowers by location and appearance. In some cases, they return directly to individual flowers on repeat visits, remembering the ones that have not been depleted of nectar and those that refill after depletion.

FLIGHT

"I never saw any other bird where the force of its wings appeared (as in a butterfly) so powerful in proportion to the weight of its body. While hovering by a flower, its tail is constantly expanded and shut like a fan, the body being kept in a nearly vertical position. This action appears to steady and support the bird, between the slow movements of its wings." — Charles Darwin, 1887

Only a few birds are known primarily by the way they fly. The dipper, for instance, "dips" in flight, diving into mountain streams in search of insects, and the eagle soars in thermal air currents. The hummingbird is unique in that it is named after its method of flight; the rapid beating of its wings produces a distinctive hum which identifies the members of its order. More like many insects than other birds, this flight includes unique hovering and darting action, changing directions "on a dime," flying backward, and even flight upside down.

Hummingbirds are able to maneuver in the air in their distinctive way not only because of their diminutive size but because of special adaptations of their anatomies. Unlike most other birds, a hummingbird wing has extremely short segments except for the outmost extensions. In most birds, these proportions are reversed, roughly corresponding to the arm of a human, with long bones in two segments of the arm and short segments in the hand. If a human arm was like that of a hummingbird, the upper and lower part of the arm would be very short, and the fingers would be the length of those two sections combined. In the hummingbird, the "hand" part of the wing is where the primary wing feathers are attached.

In the hummingbird wing, the joints between segments are not very flexible and have only a small range of motion. But the joint between the wing and the shoulder is just the opposite, with a range of motion that is almost 180 degrees. To flex the wing through this range, a very large set of muscles is attached to the hummingbird's breastbone. Almost 30 percent of the weight of a hummingbird comes from these muscles, the pectorals, the greatest percentage found in any bird. The weight of pectorals in other birds ranges from less than 10 to about 25 percent of the total body weight. The strongest of the pectorals in the hummingbird— the depressor muscles — are responsible for pulling the wing down. The muscles that raise the wing are called elevator muscles, and are half the mass of the depressors. In other birds, elevator muscles are much smaller, typically only about 10 percent of the weight of the depressors.

In other birds, raising and lowering the wings creates different kinds of action, with only the downward stroke developing lift and thrust. This is because most bird wings manipulate the wing feathers, angling them on the upward path to reduce air resistance and locking them together on the downward path, to generate the push that makes flight and forward motion possible. The hummingbird, however, does not alter the angle of the feathers between the up and down strokes. Rather, both motions are made with the feathers close together and the angle of the wing itself is changed. Different angles and patterns of up and down strokes are used to provide different kinds of flight. To move forward, the wings move in a narrow, "paddling" motion, cycling up and down in a loop pattern.

To hover, hummingbird wings paddle horizontally rather than vertically, cycling front to back roughly in the shape of a figure eight. The wings pivot during this maneuver, allowing the wing feathers to push volumes of air down while going in either direction. Depending on their weight, wing length, and the flying conditions — wind speed, humidity, altitude — hummingbird wings may cycle from twenty-two to seventy-nine times per second when hovering. The smaller the bird, the faster the beat when hovering. Some observers have measured even faster rates of beating, up to 200 times per second, during courting behavior.

In straight-ahead flight, hummingbirds are notorious for their speed. Myths and legends as well as real life observation have created the illusion that these small birds are capable of incredible feats of speed in the air. But, although they can move rapidly, hummingbirds are far from the fastest creatures in the air. Their visible speed is often exaggerated in the minds of observers because of their small size and ability to accelerate quickly. Measurements in the wild and in wind tunnels with captive hummingbirds indicate a top speed of about 30 miles per hour during prolonged, level flight. Some species may be able to fly faster for short distances or when diving, possibly up to 50 or 60 miles per hour.

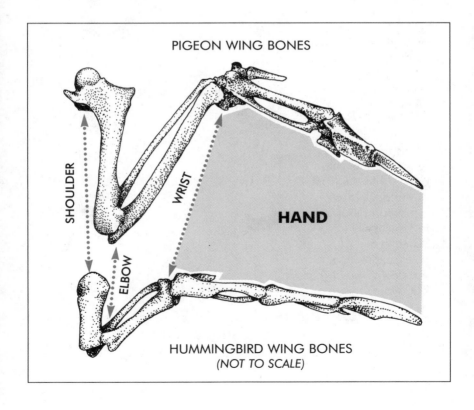

PIGEON WING BONES

SHOULDER

WRIST

ELBOW

HAND

HUMMINGBIRD WING BONES
(NOT TO SCALE)

When hovering, hummingbird wings paddle forward and back, roughly in the shape of a figure eight. The top edge of the wing always leads the bottom edge, whether the wing is going to the back or the front. At the same time, the wing is curved slightly upward, creating a downward thrust of air. If the wings are tilted to one side or the other, or to the front or the back, this thrust can be used to steer the hover in a desired direction, up, down, forward, or backward.

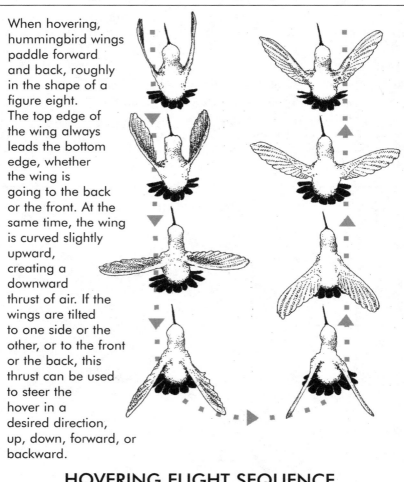

HOVERING FLIGHT SEQUENCE
TOP VIEW

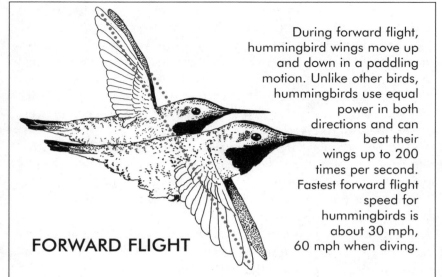

During forward flight, hummingbird wings move up and down in a paddling motion. Unlike other birds, hummingbirds use equal power in both directions and can beat their wings up to 200 times per second. Fastest forward flight speed for hummingbirds is about 30 mph, 60 mph when diving.

FORWARD FLIGHT

Hummingbirds are the only birds capable of true hovering flight. When hovering, their wings move from front to back 30–70 times per second. The smaller the hummingbird, the more beats per second. Hovering, however, requires a tremendous amount of energy, and hummingbirds will not hover any longer than is necessary.

HOVERING FLIGHT

Hummingbird wings beat at different rates according to the length of the wings and the weight of the bodies they must support. The longer the wings, the slower the beat. The largest wings on hummingbirds in North America are about 3.5" long; these wings typically beat 18–28 times per second. The smallest wings are less than 1.5" long; these beat 38–78 times per second. During some kinds of acrobatic flight or dives, hummingbirds may generate even faster rates, up to 200 times per second.

Another unique characteristic of hummingbird flight is the take-off. For other birds, flight begins slowly, with the bird jumping off a perch and flapping its wings to gain speed. For the hummingbird, its wings begin stroking before it leaves the perch. The pre-flight motion of the wings generate lift and thrust that propel the tiny hummer from rest into its normal flight speed almost instantaneously. But it is not just the effective power of the wings that allows it to take off so swiftly; the extremely small size and weight of the bird are also key factors. In landing, there is also an advantage from its small size. Hummingbirds can slow to a stop and land in an extremely short period of time — and with little impact on the landing site — because they carry so little weight and therefore generate little momentum.

CLEANING

"Among all living creatures, the hummingbird is the most beautiful in form, the most exquisite in coloration. Precious stones and metals cannot be compared with this gem of Nature. The little bird is her masterpiece."
— Georges Louis Leclerc Buffon, 1852

All birds groom their feathers on a regular basis. Feathers provide insulation and are instrumental in flight, requiring them to be clean and in good condition. Preening by hummingbirds, like most birds, is done with their bills, although they also frequently use their claws to preen feathers on their heads and necks. Preening consists of running individual feathers through a slightly open bill; the bill aligns the barbules of the feather and removes dirt and parasites.

At the same time, important feathers — wing and tail feathers required for flight — are oiled with a secretion from a gland located near the bird's tail. The uropygial gland produces an oily fluid that is spread in a thin protective coating among these feathers. After preening the hummingbird also uses its feet to clasp and scrape debris from its bill, both inside and outside. After feeding, on the other hand, the hummingbird usually resorts to the surface of a tree branch, rubbing and scraping its bill to clean it of plant material, pollen, and stray nectar that has accumulated from visits to flowers. Debris that has collected on the tongue during a preening session may be removed by scraping it against the upper surface of the bill.

Hummingbirds seek out sources of water on a regular basis, both to drink and to bathe. They prefer running water — small streams, waterfalls, or fountains — but may use the tiny quantity of moisture found on the surface of leaves for a bath. Sometimes they also take their baths "on the wing," hovering in sprays or mists of water.

REPRODUCTION

"They hang amidst fuchsia flowers, or float over beds of bromelia. They sit in their nest upon two white eggs, ready to disclose their 'golden couplets.' They dart long beaks into deep, tubular, flowers, hovering beneath the pendant bells. They poise themselves in the air, we hear not the humming of the wings, but we can almost fancy there is a voice in that beauty." — Charles Dickens, 1851

Adult hummingbirds live individually, seeking out other adults deliberately only when mating. The courtship and mating behavior varies from species to species, but follows a general pattern among North American species. The courtship and breeding season is timed to provide an abundant source of food for mothers and young birds. In North America, this can be anytime from early spring through summer. The exceptions are the Anna's hummingbird and the Allen's hummingbird. These species breed earlier, from December through the spring months, probably because some do not migrate, but spend the winter in the breeding area, the warmer parts of southern California.

Sometimes hummingbirds may have more than one breeding cycle in a year. This is often related to the abundance or scarcity of local food supplies, which in turn is related to weather patterns. Some North American hummingbirds may also restart the breeding process — including nest building — if the eggs or young from the first round are destroyed. Ruby-throated, black-chinned, and white-eared hummingbirds may also sometimes begin a second breeding period before the first brood has flown the nest. In these cases, the female usually begins constructing a second nest while still feeding the first batch.

Male hummingbirds may attract females because of their bright plumage and aggressive behavior, but courtship is initiated by females. Before mating begins, the males of most species stake out territories for feeding and attracting females. Male hummingbirds usually migrate north earlier than females in order to do this.

At the beginning of their reproductive season, females choose nesting sites and begin building their nests. When a female has completed a nest, she begins a hunt for a suitable male. In many cases, however, this does not mean comparing the plumage or behavior of competing males, but simply selecting the first one she encounters in her search.

Males have specific mating behavior that includes a variety of poses, flight patterns, and sounds generated by voice and feathers. When perching, the males of some species also open their wings in unique stretching poses. Also while perched, they may move their bills in unison with females, or make mock feeding gestures. On the wing, male hummingbirds typically exhibit steep aggressive dives during courtship periods and also perform "shuttle flights," darting back and forth in front of the female. Some observers have noted that male hummingbirds are often deliberate about the direction in which they make these display flights. With their bodies pointing toward the sun, the light creates a brighter spectacle as it reflects and refracts off of their iridescent plumage. In fact, ideal hummingbird territories are usually those where open space permits the best viewing of such performances.

During any of this behavior, most male hummingbirds use vocal calls that they reserve for this occasion. In general, males are more vocal when their habitats consist of darker, denser vegetation. In some species, the males typically group together in informal colonies, called leks, for mating purposes. In North America, the blue-throated hummingbird is the only species — except a few which are occasional visitors — that exhibits this behavior. In leks, the males are much more vocal than when single, creating what are called "singing assemblies," with the voices of many males massed together, although this is not in harmony.

Another source of mating sounds comes from the unique flight habits of the hummingbirds. Their normal "hum," made from the rapid beating of their wings, can be modified during flights or hovering to create a number of special sounds, including whistles, booms, chatters, and rattles.

Some biologists have suggested that most or all of the ritualized courtship behavior of male hummingbirds may actually be simple aggression, the male defending his territory against an intruder. In the breeding season, the female is considered just another intruder, with instinctive mating activity occurring only after the female refuses to be chased off. In some hummingbird species in South America, in fact, male hummingbirds have frequently been observed mounting other males, females of other species, and even leaves. And, with some exceptions, the behavior used by male hummingbirds to defend their territories is similar to that used when courting females.

Mating by hummingbirds is a brief act of copulation, with the male mounting the female for a few seconds. Multiple mountings may occur over a period of a few hours, but the mating does not last more than one day after a female has encountered a male. Including the courtship display and copulation, the total time male and female hummingbirds are together may last less than five minutes.

Unlike all other birds, male hummingbirds are only part of the reproductive cycle during mating. After the female has mated, the male has nothing more to do with hatching the eggs, or the feeding and protection of the young birds. A very few exceptions to this rule have been observed by ornithologists with individual male hummingbirds. But this lack of fatherly support is more than made up by the care provided by mother hummingbirds. From the selection of the nest site to the feeding of the young birds, female hummingbirds are attentive parents. This includes protection of the nest. Females with nests are extremely aggressive birds, charging and

Courtship behavior by male hummingbirds includes diving, hovering, and "shuttling" in front of their audience, usually accompanied by loud wing sounds.

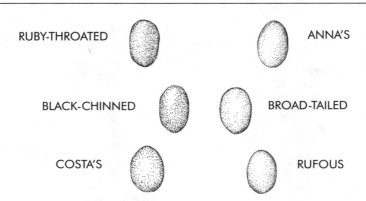

RUBY-THROATED   ANNA'S

BLACK-CHINNED   BROAD-TAILED

COSTA'S   RUFOUS

Hummingbird eggs are the smallest of all bird eggs. All of the North American hummingbird species lay white eggs that vary slightly in size and shape. Eggs shown are actual size.

chasing any animal that may be a threat, including birds as large as eagles.

Everything about the hummingbird is small, including the time required to lay eggs and hatch them. The average incubation period for North American species is 16 days. All hummingbirds lay two eggs, with rare exceptions. Eggs for every species, including those in South America, are white in color and resemble elongated ovals in shape. Although these eggs are the smallest laid by any of the world's birds, they are at the same time the largest in comparison to the mother bird's size. Hummingbird eggs at the time they are laid represent about 10 percent of the mother bird's body. In actual size, they would be too small to pass as jelly beans.

Most of the time, the female will lay her eggs in the morning hours. The time period between the laying of the first egg and the second is usually two full days, or 48 hours. However, some females have been observed laying a second egg in only 24 hours and others may take up to three days. The female begins incubating them as soon as the first one is laid. The period of incubation varies among species, from nine to twenty days, with most species in North America requiring 15–17 days.

Incubation of the eggs requires the mother to provide a constant temperature in order to safeguard the development of the embryos. The temperature of the air, however, may be higher or lower than this level — about 90 degrees F. — requiring the mother to be able to either warm or cool the eggs at different times. Warming is achieved by contact with her "brood patch," an area of the chest where there are no feathers, allowing the eggs to directly contact the heat of her body. The insulation of her feathers and the nest material also provide protection against the cold. When daytime temperature get too high, the female may leave the eggs exposed and if necessary, use her body to block the direct heat from the sun. Like all bird eggs, hummingbird eggs are turned at regular intervals to maintain even heat.

Because of their high metabolism, female hummingbirds must leave eggs unattended frequently in order to feed. During incubation, however, they typically spend less time feeding than at other times of the year. Observers have noted that female hummingbirds may leave the nest many times during a day, with as many as 100 or more absences, but the total time spent at the nest still ranges from 60 to 80 percent of all daylight hours. Other factors may temporarily force a mother bird off the nest — most often the intrusion of other birds or predators.

Most baby hummingbirds hatch without feathers (a few species have an irregular coat of down), are completely blind, and lack the one most characteristic feature of their parents, long bills. But like all birds, they are immediately capable of eating and mother birds begin providing food just after they hatch. This feeding consists of the mother regurgitating food from her crop — mostly small insects — directly into the throat and crop of the babies. Baby hummingbirds in the nest are often observed with larger, protrud-

Hummingbird chicks are born blind, without feathers, and
with tiny, unformed bills.

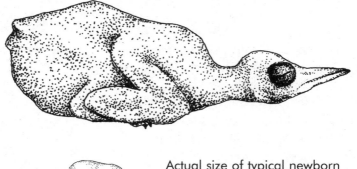

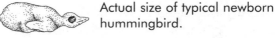

Actual size of typical newborn
hummingbird.

ing necks, evidence of the food stuffed in their crops. Unlike adults,
baby hummingbirds have a reddish lining to their bills, thought to
help stimulate feeding behavior from the mother bird. The young-
sters may in turn be stimulated to beg for food by the sound of the
mother bird's wings. Feeding sessions do not take long. Both chicks
are usually fed in a session that averages 30–50 seconds.

Baby hummingbirds are nestbound for an average of 20 days,
with an extreme of about 30 days. During this period, the mother
frequently leaves the nest to gather food, bringing back take-home
meals for the nestlings several times per hour. At night during the
nesting stage, mother birds do not enter a state of torpor. Although
this is the usual response to chilly temperatures, avoiding this state
allows them to provide extra warmth to their young. Baby hummingbirds have also proven to be well-adapted to temperature fluc-
tuations before they develop their first set of feathers, usually by the
second or third week of life.

Young hummingbirds fly for the first time at about 20 days. At this time, their feathers are not yet fully grown, and they may still be fed by their mother. Mother hummingbirds may continue feeding their young for up to 40–65 days, with the actual period of support related to local feeding conditions.

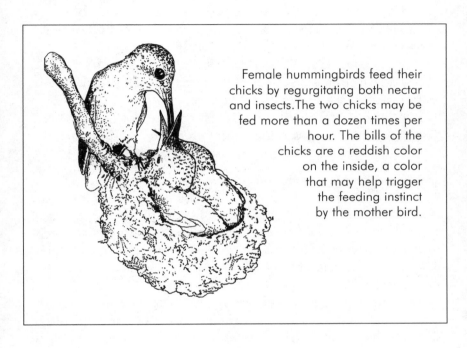

Female hummingbirds feed their chicks by regurgitating both nectar and insects. The two chicks may be fed more than a dozen times per hour. The bills of the chicks are a reddish color on the inside, a color that may help trigger the feeding instinct by the mother bird.

NESTS

"Upon an examination of the nest, I was not surprised at my discerning it with difficulty from the other moss that grew on the tree, for the outside has a coating of green moss, such as is commonly on old pales, enclosures, and old trees; the nest, as well as the bird, is the least of all others; that which I have taken is round, and the inside is of a brown and quite soft down, which seems to have been collected from the stems of the sumach, which are covered with a soft wool of this color, and the plant grows in great abundance here; the inner diameter of the nest is hardly a geometrical inch at the top, and depth scarcely half an inch." — Thomas Anburey, 1789

Hummingbird nests are some of the most complex constructions created by birds. This is partly because the materials these tiny creatures use are more limited than those of other birds; the birds' small size forces them to select only minute, lightweight components. The nest building is also limited to the efforts of female hummingbirds only; males have nothing to do with the construction or site selection.

Nests are constructed in two layers. The outer layer is made from a variety of natural elements, including twigs, grasses, animal fur, slivers of bark, moss, lichen, and leaves. Usually, but not always, hummingbirds raid spiders' webs for supplies of silk that is used to bind nesting materials together. Other silk-like materials may also be used, including fine fibers from plants and animal underfur. An inner layer completes the nest construction. This section is a lining made from available materials that provide a soft cushion for support and insulation. Lining materials may come from dry, fluffy vegetation such as cottonwood silk, molted feathers from other birds, or clumps of fur shed by mammals. Some species of hummingbirds

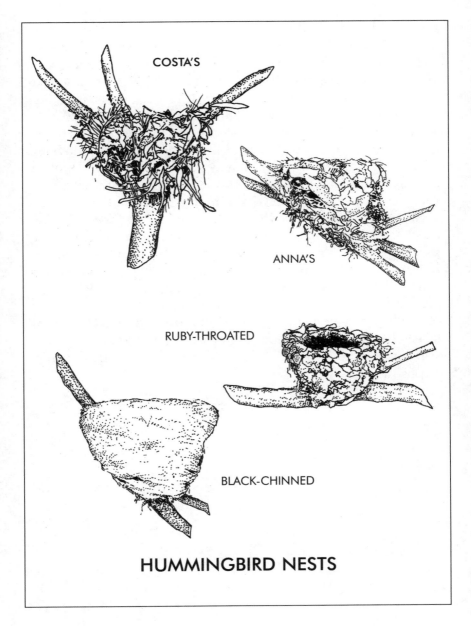

COSTA'S

ANNA'S

RUBY-THROATED

BLACK-CHINNED

HUMMINGBIRD NESTS

also seem to practice thievery in the construction of their nests —
the females raid the old and new nest sites of females of their own
and other species for materials to use in their own nests. Hummingbirds nesting in the vicinity of human habitation will also take
advantage of human-generated materials for their nests, including
hair from humans and their pets, dryer lint, and fabric scraps.

Hummingbird nests are not easy to spot because the materials
they are made from usually blend in well with the surroundings.
Some hummingbirds also deliberately add camouflage to the outer
nest, including bits of moss, lichen, and bark. The nest itself is flexible, and expands as the tiny eggs turn into chicks and grow in size.

Nest building may be started and finished in less than a day, but
most nests require from several days to a week or more of work. In
some cases, weather and interruptions for feeding may stretch this
time to a week or more. On occasion, females have been observed
adding to their nests after they have laid eggs. A few of the hummingbird species in North America are also known for their habit
of building new nests on top of existing nests. In addition, many
female hummingbirds return to established nesting sites year after
year, but they rarely use the same nest without complete or partial
reconstruction.

MORTALITY

"... for the pleasure which I experience on seeing a Humming Bird is as great at the present moment as when first I saw one. During the first 20 years of my acquaintance with these wonderful works of creation my thoughts were often directed to them in the day, and my night dreams have not unfrequently carried me to their native forests in the distant country of America." — John Gould, 1861

Hummingbirds, like many small animals, are at the low end of a feeding chain, preyed upon by a wide range of larger animals. But despite the threat this predation poses, most hummingbird deaths come from causes other than being eaten. Disease, parasites, malnutrition, exhaustion, dehydration, and cold weather take a far greater toll on hummingbird populations than predators.

Although hummingbirds may be aggressive when defending their territory, their small size makes them vulnerable to predators. One of the biggest menaces may be from small hawks — sparrow hawks or sharp-shinned hawks, for example — which are agile enough to catch this elusive prey. Hummingbirds can also be attacked by other birds, including crows, orioles, and roadrunners.

Danger from the ground can include frogs, snakes, and lizards. There have also been reports of hummingbirds caught by predatory fish such as bass, when they make the mistake of flying too close to the surface of a body of water. Even insects can successfully catch hummingbirds in some cases. A record exists of a praying mantis attacking a ruby-throated hummingbird, and observers have seen dragonflies catch hummingbirds, but these insects are not typically a danger. Some spiders, however, take advantage of hummingbirds if they get entangled in a web, a constant danger for some species because they use spiderweb silk in making nests.

Although not common, hummingbirds may also be threatened by the natural hazards found in vegetation. Thorns, spikes, and bristles on some plants can become entangled in their feathers, causing injury or death.

The greatest hazards to hummingbirds, however, generally come from contact with humans. Window glass is a chief culprit in many deaths and injuries, an invisible obstacle found in close proximity to many of their feeding sites. Window and door screens have also been known to stun and kill hummingbirds, and cases have been reported of hummingbirds with their beaks jammed into screens too tightly for the birds to release themselves.

Hummingbird eggs and nestlings are threatened by an even greater range of dangers. Tree squirrels, rats, mice, and other rodents raid nests for an easy meal, as do many birds, including jays and crows. Tree-climbing snakes, frogs, and lizards are also on the hunt for such a source of food. Some insects that are not a threat to adult hummingbirds can injure or kill their young. Ants, particularly fire ants, are such a threat.

Diseases that affect hummingbirds may be passed on by contact with other birds of their own or different species and from insects such as mosquitoes, lice, and fleas. A major threat comes from specialized lice that target birds. Chewing bird lice are typical of these tiny crawling insects that frequently infest feathers. Other predators that may prey on the blood of hummingbirds include mites, ticks, louse flies, and Hemiptera. Internally, hummingbirds may be infected with tapeworms, roundworms, flukes, and other parasitic animals.

The tiny hummingbird also has a fragile link to life because of its tremendous requirement for food. Severe weather conditions, the variability of local food supplies, and destruction of prime natural habitat all have a negative impact on its health. The lifespan of a hummingbird, however, can be relatively lengthy. Observations of banded birds and records of hummingbirds kept in captivity show that they may live up to ten or more years. But in the wild in North America most hummingbirds do not live this long. Measurement of mortality from census studies of banded birds show that these birds probably experience a survival rate of between 25–50 percent per year. As with many other birds and animals, the greatest threat to life comes at the earliest ages. Hummingbird nests, despite their efficient construction and camouflage, are vulnerable to many predators and the forces of nature. Only 20 to 50 percent of young birds survive to leave the nest.

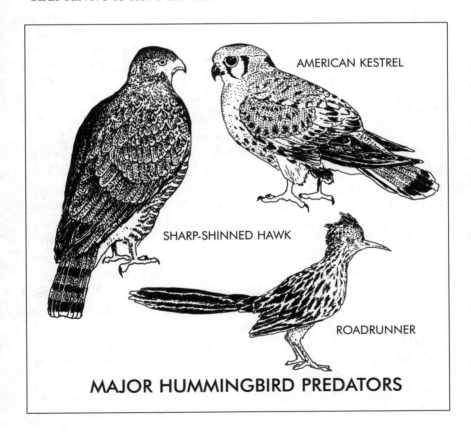

AMERICAN KESTREL

SHARP-SHINNED HAWK

ROADRUNNER

MAJOR HUMMINGBIRD PREDATORS

POLLINATION

"Almost always on the wing, we scarcely see them in any other position. Living on the honeyed sweets of the most beautiful flowers, and the minute insects concealed in their corollas, they come to us as etherial beings, and it is not surprising that they should have excited the wonder and admiration of mankind." — Reverend John Bachman, 1840

Nectar is the primary food of hummingbirds but it is not given up by flowers without a benefit in return. As hummingbirds and insects acquire this high energy food, they help spread pollen from one flower to another, allowing flowers to pollinate and create new generations of plants.

Plants have developed a wide variety of colorful and aromatic signs — flowers — to attract hummingbirds and insects. In North America, most of the flowers that are pollinated by birds are red — insects are unable to distinguish this color — and are not heavy scent producers. But hummingbirds do not always use color to find food. Experiments with two species, black-chinned and ruby-throated hummingbirds, have shown that they do not inherit any special instinct that attracts them to colors, but develop a memory for identifying the location of nectar sources from practice after finding them. Even so, hummingbirds — in fact, all birds — are most sensitive to those colors in the spectrum that have the longest wavelengths, which are the red hues.

Once located, hummingbirds generally stick with the same sources, seeking out similar flowers for more of the same nectar. This behavior benefits the flowers, because if the birds' preferences were random, the pollen picked up from one flower would be less likely to end up in another flower of the same species.

Pollination by hummingbirds also presents plants with another challenge. If they develop flowers that have the high sugar content

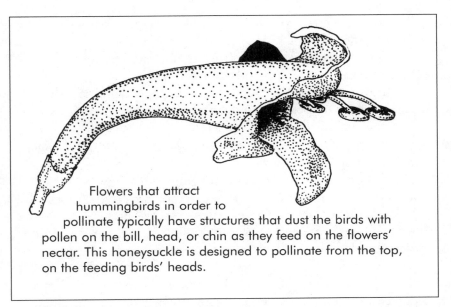

Flowers that attract hummingbirds in order to pollinate typically have structures that dust the birds with pollen on the bill, head, or chin as they feed on the flowers' nectar. This honeysuckle is designed to pollinate from the top, on the feeding birds' heads.

needed by hummingbirds, this nectar might be consumed by insects before hummingbirds can get to it, and most insects are much less efficient at spreading pollen than hummingbirds. The solution for these flowers is a lack of odor — a powerful attraction for insects — and red coloring that is poorly perceived by insects' eyes.

Unlike the hummingbirds of South America, North American species have bills that are closely matched in length and shape. The flowers available to North American hummingbirds are also much more similar in size and shape than those found in South America. In the north, hummingbirds of different species are more likely to share feeding preferences than in South America, where the bills of some species have developed unique shapes to extract nectar from specific species of flowers. And consequently, some flowers found in South America are pollinated only by a single species of humming-bird.

Plants that have developed flowers that are primarily pollinated by birds have been divided into five different types, distinguished by general shape. These include:

- gullet flowers (long tubes, upper lip overhanging)
- tubular flowers (long tubes)
- brush flowers (clustered in a spherical or cylindrical shape)
- capitula (clustered in a hemispherical shape)
- spurred flowers (tubes formed by separate petals)

In North America, three of these types are native: the gullet, tubular, and spurred flowers.

Plants that are pollinated by hummingbirds have evolved to make this process work efficiently. Beginning with the nature of the flowers, plants are usually frequented more by hummingbirds than insects. This is because the color of the flower and the lack of scent make the plant less conspicuous to insects, especially bees. The flowers of bee-pollinated plants are often constructed differently, providing a convenient landing platform for the insect, which rarely feeds on nectar while hovering. Hummingbird flowers usually feature long, narrow passages between the nectar and the outside, making the nectar less accessible to insects. Because hummingbirds are heavier than insects, the flowers they feed on are also usually stronger, featuring petals and other flower parts made of thicker tissue, and thus less likely to be damaged by the feeding action of the birds. Thicker, tougher tissue may also prevent nectar from being "highjacked" through the side or base of the flower. The gentle extraction of nectar by the hummingbird's tongue ensures the flower a longer life so it can continue producing nectar, and thus attract additional pollination.

Flowers transfer their pollen to hummingbirds through contact. As they hover and insert their bills into flowers, the bills and heads of the birds brush against stamens, the pollen-carrying structures of the flowers. Flower species have different designs for stamens and where the stamens are located. But in hummingbird flowers, the design and position always ensures that pollen will be picked up in the act of feeding. In some of these flowers, the pollen is brushed off by the birds' heads as they hover under a flower; in others the pollen dusts off onto the chin. Pollen may be contacted by the base of the bill, the tip of the bill, the top or bottom of the bill, or more than one location. The hummingbird carries the pollen with it as it visits other flowers of the same species, depositing some of the pollen by the same feeding action.

Flowers that have developed primarily to attract hummingbirds may feature several types of basic structures, including separate petals, long tubes, or clumps of tubes.

VOCALIZATION

"Hummingbirds are not supposed to sing, but to use their voices for squeaking when angry or frightened."
— Anna Botsford Comstock, 1911

What the hummingbird offers to the observer in beauty of plumage is not well-matched in the attractiveness of its voice. Although a few hummingbird species have pleasant, multi-note phrases, none have what could be called a dramatic song, and most produce distinctly nonmusical notes when they vocalize. Both males and females of most species are known to make frequent calls as they feed, usually single or multiple "chipping" sounds. When confronting trespassers or involved in courtship displays, however, males usually become noisier.

Hummingbirds also are unique among birds because they frequently use the sound of their wings to generate specific sounds used for communicating. These variations in wing hum are usually produced when confronting interlopers, but they may also be part of the courtship flights of males. Wing sounds include explosive pops, thumps, variable-pitched hums, whistles, and rattles.

FOR MORE HELP

Recordings of bird calls are collected and analyzed at the Cornell Laboratory of Ornithology (Ithaca, NY). Audio tapes and compact discs are available from this collection, including most of the hummingbirds found in North America. More information is available on the World Wide Web at
<http://www.ornith.cornell.edubirdlab.html>

Tapes and CDs can be found at local bookstores, published by:
Peterson Field Guides/Houghton Mifflin Company
120 Beacon Street, Somerville, MA 02143

HUMMINGBIRD CALLS

SPECIES	CALL
ALLEN'S	single and multiple notes, multi-note trill
ANNA'S	soft, scratchy, squeaky chatter and single sharp "chrp"
BLACK-CHINNED	single note or chatter, also multi-note warble
BLUE-THROATED	short, high-pitched musical "theep"
BROAD-BILLED	low-pitched, strong chatter, "grrk, grrk"
BROAD-TAILED	soft, squeak-like notes, "chrp, chrp" and squeaky chatter
BUFF-BELLIED	multi-note, short sharp "tchp, tchp, tchp"
CALLIOPE	soft, single notes "tik, tik"
COSTA'S	high-pitched, quiet chattering "chip, chip, chip"
LUCIFER	single note "tic, tic, tic"
MAGNIFICENT	single notes, musical "peep"
RUBY-THROATED	single, multiple notes, and chatter "chrp, chrp"
RUFOUS	single and multiple notes, extended squeaky "tcheeep, tcheeep"
VIOLET-CROWNED	metallic single notes and chatter, "chip, chip, chip"
WHITE-EARED	soft bell-like "tink, tink, tink"

TERRITORY

"Strangely enough, these beautiful little creatures are possessed of a most unfortunate disposition, which frequently leads them to attack any bird they fancy is trespassing on their domain. They know no fear, and with equal courage rush at one of their kind or a passing Hawk."
— R. Ridgway, 1892

Hummingbirds are noted for their aggressive defense of territory. During the season when certain flowers are in bloom, individual hummingbirds may "stake out" the area around certain bushes or trees, chasing off other hummingbirds, other species of birds, and even insects if they trespass. For some trees and bushes, more than one hummingbird may have distinct territorial zones, with a few square yards enough to define their individual zones. These zones may also shift frequently, as one plant ends its blooming phase and another begins.

In North America, the defense of territory is less characteristic for hummingbirds than in South America. Also, not all hummingbirds are territorial or defend territory at all times. In general, of all the hummingbird species, those that have the brightest, most iridescent colors are the most territorial, and those that have the most muted, drab colors are the least. Attacks in defense of territory are mostly bluff, with the attacking birds making the loudest wing "hums" they can as they dive at intruders. Frequent and persistent diving generally has a positive effect, but some cases have been observed of defending hummingbirds pecking and stabbing at other birds — usually other hummingbirds — with their bills.

Territory is critical to hummingbirds because it defines the amount of food available to them, food that must be ingested frequently in order to keep up with the tremendous demands for energy created by their high-speed metabolisms. Wherever food sources are located, territory may be staked out and defended. This includes bird feeders. Hummingbird feeders with more than one opening, and yards with more than one feeder, may attract more than one regular visitor, and these backyard feeding stations are frequently subdivided by hummingbirds into individual feeding zones, defended vigorously against interlopers.

In one study, rufous hummingbirds in western North America used complex feeding patterns to take maximum advantage of their territories. Evidence from this study shows that the outermost fringe of each hummingbird's territory is the hardest to defend, as it covers more area and permits more opportunities for sneak attacks by other birds. As a countermeasure, at the beginning of each day, hummingbirds feed first from flowers in the outer perimeters of their territory, working their way during the day toward the center of their territory. With the outermost plants temporarily depleted of nectar, there is less chance that raids by other hummingbirds will have a negative impact on their supply of food, and the smaller, inner portion of the territory is easier to defend.

Although the defense of territory is obviously logical for the hummingbird, it is an instinctive behavior. The defense of its territory makes a hummingbird attack just about any living thing that intrudes, from humans to large predatory birds that could easily eat the smaller bird. Attacks are often related, however, to the size of territory, the number of competing hummingbirds in the area, and the availability of food within the territory. When nectar is scarce, the hummingbird may defend the territory less vigorously, a reaction that saves valuable energy. When nectar is gone, some hummingbirds may still defend the territory, a phenomenon frequently noted around empty hummingbird feeders.

Most of the hummingbirds found in North America are migratory, visiting only from spring through late summer or fall. As they migrate to and from Mexico and Central America, territories are rarely established or defended, mostly because the birds do not stay long in one place. In some locations, however, temporary territories may be created when significant sources of nectar are located on the travel route.

Both males and females may have feeding territories, but females also establish defensive territories when nesting. When protecting their eggs or young, females exhibit the same bold approach as the most aggressive males, attacking any moving object that comes too close.

Territorial protection, however, is sometimes just a daytime behavior. In parts of South America and in some hummingbird colonies in captivity, rival birds will roost together at night on the same branches, a practice that helps defend against a common enemy, the cold.

THE FASHION
OF FEATHERS

*"The humbird for some queen's rich cage more fit,
Than in the vacant wilderness to sit."* — William Wood, 1634

Hummingbirds do not always fare well when placed in contact with humans. Although they receive tremendous benefit from ornamental plantings, fruit trees, flowers, and gardens planted as part of an expanding civilization — and many participants in this expansion also put out feeders for hummingbirds and other birds — this civilization expands at the expense of forests, wetlands, prairies, and other natural habitats.

Most of the woodlands that once covered the eastern part of the continent are now replaced by farmland, pastures, roads, and the sprawl of cities. This has left fewer breeding and nesting opportunities for the ruby-throated hummingbird, the only species that thrives in this region, although its numbers are not yet threatened by the loss of habitat. Other species, however, suffer when stands of sheltering trees, flowering shrubs, or other useful vegetation are removed or replaced; especially for hummingbirds that are "trapliners" — those that typically feed in long, connected aerial paths from one food source to another. For these birds, intermittent breaks in their natural grazing patterns may reduce their ability to survive.

In the 1800s, a greater threat from civilization was posed by the use of hummingbird feathers — and even entire hummingbird bodies — as ornaments on women's hats, dresses, and in jewelry. Trends in the fashion industry in the late 1800s made bird feathers a hot item and resulted in the widespread hunting and trapping of species with the most iridescent plumage. An investigation by an ornithologist in 1886 determined that at least forty different American bird

"The new hats will be laden with plumage almost to the exclusion of flowers ... To make up the feather ornaments boxes of birds are imported, the feathers are stripped from their wings and breasts, and are pasted together in bands and coronets, and new colorings are thus made up. There are whole boxes filled with tourterelles — meek little doves in their solemn drab shades; smaller cases contain dozens of tiny humming-birds; while great wooden chests are filled with brilliant impions that are as large as turkeys, and are only found on the highest mountain peaks; many of the green-blue feathers and those of flame-colors are taken from these mammoth birds. ... The breasts of humming-birds form medallions on flame-colored impion turbans."

Harper's Bazar
September 3, 1881

species were used to feather fashionable hats and garments; about 75 percent of the hats checked by that observer used feathers as ornaments. As the fashion trend spread, ever more exotic birds were sought after and the iridescent plumage of the hummingbird became a particularly hot item. At about the same time, beginning in the early 1800s, a "great age" of discovery in natural history spread through the major countries in Europe, culminating in grand expositions and displays in the mid-part of the century.

The Great Exhibition of 1851 in London was one such extravaganza, showcasing the latest technology and scientific knowledge of the time. One of the greatest attractions at this fair was the first ever public display of preserved hummingbirds, collected by the eminent British ornithologist John Gould, who at the time had not seen a live hummingbird in the wild. The thousands of birds in his collection were solicited and organized from his residence across the Atlantic Ocean from where these birds naturally occurred. In a special building constructed just for this event, 320 hummingbird species were presented in glass cases and succeeded in awing thousands of visitors, including much of the royalty of England and the continent. The result was a heightened interest in the unique plumage of these birds, and a desire by fashionable people to "own" a piece of this natural creature. Even before birds attracted the attentions of milliners and dress designers, rich bird collectors vied with each other for rare and exotic specimens.

Fashion illustrations from *Harper's Bazar* magazine (1885 and 1886) featuring designs made with hummingbirds, their feathers, and feathers from other exotic birds.

As the fashion in feathered wear spread, some designers used bird wings and even entire birds as part of their decorative schemes, including hummingbirds perched on artificial flowers. Stuffed hummingbirds also appeared on aigrettes (ornamental attachments pinned to hats), feathered fans, garnitures (ornamental displays pinned to dresses), and elaborate pieces of jewelry. At the peak of this trend, several million hummingbirds were killed annually to supply the demand for feathers, not including even larger quantities of herons, egrets, kingfishers, birds of paradise, lyre birds, parrots, woodpeckers, larks, gulls, and osprey. On March 21, 1888, a single auction in London recorded the sale of 12,000 hummingbird skins; the total for the year in that city alone exceeded 400,000. These skins were shipped out of South America, mostly from Rio de Janeiro, and major ports in North America.

The trend continued for several decades, peaking just after the turn of the century. Between 1904 and 1911, according to records of feather auctions in London, 152,000 hummingbirds were imported from North America to make hats. In an earlier year, a single dealer is reported to have purchased more than 400,000 hummingbirds from just one source in the West Indies.

How was the tremendous demand for hummingbird skins met? Bird hunters had to sharpen their skills in order to bag hummingbirds. Many of the species most desired were not elusive but their tiny size made them difficult to shoot, at least without destroying the bird's bodies in the process. Hunters with rifles used small shot or bullets, although some believed that the smallest ammunition size was not appropriate because it penetrated the body. Instead, they preferred a medium-sized shot or bullet, which killed the bird by smashing it, but didn't destroy the feathered skin. Other hunters switched to firing small water-filled balloons made from animal intestines or other material. Natives recruited to gather hummingbirds, at least in South America, often preferred blowguns and their skill was often sufficient to hit the tiny targets in flight. Mesh nets made of fine thread were often employed, and were very effective when placed around flowering trees where multiple territories were held by rival male hummingbirds. In the Caribbean islands, another method was also popular. There, glue made from plant sources was used to coat target branches and flower groups; feeding hummingbirds would stick to their food source.

In the pueblo cultures of America, priests and other tribal figures who required hummingbird feathers for rituals got them with special trapping techniques. They used long, thin fibers — horsehair was preferred after these animals were introduced to the region — to form nooses that were placed around the blossoms of the Rocky Mountain bee plant.

The craze for hummingbird feathers, however, was not without its critics. Ornithologists, amateur bird watchers, nature lovers, social commentators, and others were public and vociferous in their objections. The bird-watching public, in particular, found much to fault with the trend, and gradually built up organizations and political clout to deal with it. In Great Britain, the Royal Society for the Protection of Birds, and in the United States, the Audubon Society, were formed to end the exploitation of birds for fashion. These early conservationist movements were originally the work of wealthy and prominent citizens, but their public statements and the example they set helped influence the general public to adopt a different attitude about nature and its preservation.

By the beginning of the twentieth century, local Audubon groups in several parts of the country had generated cooperative pledges with milliners to voluntarily restrict the importation and use of some kinds of feathers, including hummingbirds. Although these agreements were not universal — and, in fact, were not always adhered to by the companies that had signed them — they were part of a general movement that established a new concept of respect and appreciation for winged creatures and other animals.

ALIEN VISITORS

"There is a curious bird to see to, called a humming bird, no bigger then a great Beetle." — Thomas Morton, 1637

M ost birding experts believe the current status of hummingbirds in North America involves 15 species, only those birds that not only arrive here every year, but regularly breed while they are here. Other hummingbird species, however, occasionally visit, and there is some evidence that over time, additional species may become more permanent. Visiting species include:

- Bahama woodstar *Calliphlox evelynae*
- berylline *Amazilia beryllina*
- Cuban emerald *Chlorostilbon ricordii*
- green violet-eared *Colibri thalassinus*
- plain-capped starthroat *Heliomaster constantii*
- rufous-tailed *Amazilia tzacatl*
- Xantus *Hylocharis xantusii*

ON DISPLAY

Hummingbird junkies may need more than a backyard feeder to fill their appetite for these birds. Maximum exposure for hummingbirds is provided at a number of wildlife preserves in the southwest, a few zoos with resident hummingbirds, and at the only hummingbird aviary in North America, the Arizona-Sonora Desert Museum.

Arizona-Sonora Desert Museum
2021 North Kinney Road, Tucson, AZ 85743
1-520-883-2702

MIGRATION

"That our enthusiasm and excitement with regard to most things become lessened, if not deadened, by time, particularly when we have acquired what we vainly consider a complete knowledge of the subject, is, I fear, too often the case with most of us; not so, however, I believe, with those who take up the study of the family of Humming Birds."
— John Gould, 1861

Most of the hummingbirds of North America are unique from the species in South America in that they are migratory. Twice a year, in the spring and the fall, these birds fly between their southern wintering territory and their northern breeding territory. Depending on the geographical location, this migration may begin and end over a period of a few months.

In some areas of North America, migration routes for different species will overlap, and the routes for others will narrow considerably, mostly forced by the availability of food and the environmental conditions. In the canyons of southern Arizona and New Mexico, southern Florida and the Florida Keys, and coastal areas of the Gulf states, primarily Texas, large numbers of hummingbirds of different species may congregate during these periods, providing enhanced observing conditions for bird lovers.

Migration flight can be extremely stressful for hummingbirds, as they have little capacity for storing energy. During migration, they are more vulnerable to predators, disease, starvation, and freezing. Ruby-throated hummingbirds regularly migrate across large expanses of the Caribbean Sea and are particularly threatened. The rufous hummingbird has the distinction of the longest migration route, more than 2,000 miles. Other species may migrate only a few hundred miles, and some Allen's, Anna's, and Costa's hummingbirds live year-round north of the Mexican border.

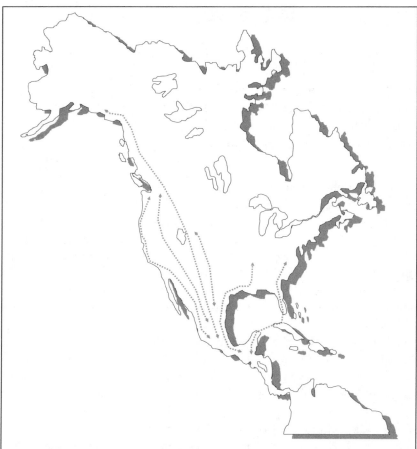

HUMMINGBIRD MIGRATION ROUTES

Different species of hummingbirds traditionally follow the same routes between their breeding territory and their wintering territory. Some routes overlap and some species have more than one route. Some ruby-throated hummingbirds, the most common species in eastern North America, fly at least part of their migration routes over the Caribbean Sea.

BACKYARD HUMMINGBIRDS

"Yet by some object ev'ry brain is stirr'd,
The dull may waken to a humming-bird."
— Alexander Pope, 1742

B irds are rarely as accommodating as hummingbirds for backyard nature lovers. These hovering creatures are well-pleased with the addition of nectar feeders, which they quickly discover and frequent with regularity. Gardeners have also added to the backyard bounty for hummingbirds by planting trees, bushes, and flowers that produce nectar for their diet.

Natural supplies of nectar from backyard plantings and sugar-water from feeders are also appropriate additions to the environment with which hummingbirds must contend. Diminishing native habitats — a consequence of the expansion of human presence in North America — has created a situation that places increasing pressure on hummingbirds in their quest for survival, pressure that may be relieved with artifical feeding stations and planted vegetation. Especially during migration, hummingbirds require plentiful opportunities to obtain food, opportunities that have been interrupted by the spread of civilization.

Hummingbird feeders are now widely available in retail stores and by mail order. Some bird lovers have had decades of experience using these liquid dispensers, and some hummingbirds return year after year to the same feeders.

To dye or not to dye? Hummingbird feeders were traditionally filled with sugar water dyed red. The red dye was considered an instrumental element in attracting these birds, but the coloring was often made from chemicals that could cause serious health problems, for humans if not for birds. Even with newer, safer dyes,

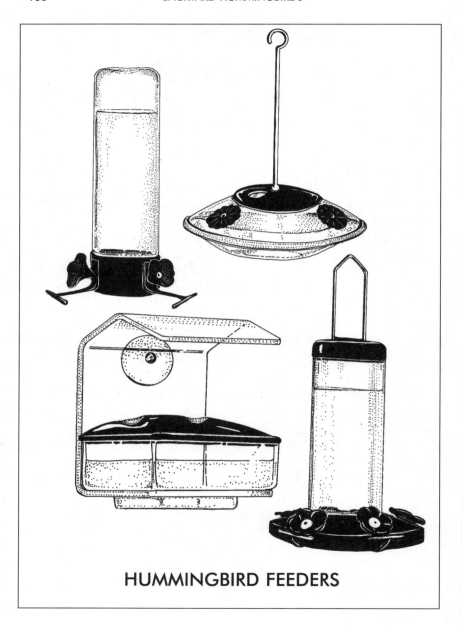

HUMMINGBIRD FEEDERS

HUMMINGBIRD GARDENS

Hummingbird lovers may increase their enjoyment by creating an environment that is beneficial and attractive to these birds. Annuals, perennials, trees, and bushes that feature nectar-rich flowers can be planted in most geographic zones in North America. Experts advise using non-hybrid plants, however, as some hybrids may not produce nectar. Recommended plantings include:

TREES azalea, flowering quince, lantana, manzanita, mimosa, red buckeye

BUSHES AND VINES coral honeysuckle, japanese honeysuckle, morning glory, trumpet creeper

FLOWERS bee balm, hollyhock, penstemon, lupine, canna, cardinal flower, columbine, four-o'clock, yucca, fire spike, shrimp plant, petunia, jacobinia, impatien, fuchsia, red salvia, scarlet sage, jewelweed

---

WARNING!

The use of pesticides is a double threat to hummingbirds. They can ingest these chemicals while collecting nectar, and the use of pesticides kills many of the insects that are a necessary source of protein for hummingbirds.

FOR MORE INFORMATION

Hummingbird Gardens, by Nancy Newfield and Barbara Nielsen. Available from local bookstores or the publisher (Chapters Publishing Ltd, Shelburne, Vermont).

FEEDER RECIPE RULES

- Recommended solution:
  1 part white sugar + 4 parts water
  or
  1 part white sugar + 5 parts water
- Use bottled water or boil water (cool before using)
- No food coloring is acceptable
- Honey is not a recommended substitute for sugar
- No sugar substitutes are acceptable
- Clean feeders weekly; more often in hot weather (use hot water but NO soap to clean)
- Clean and refill feeders if solution becomes cloudy
- Empty and clean feeders before refilling
- For convenience, make large batches and refrigerate

however, there may be problems when used in liquids consumed by hummingbirds. These creatures ingest so much liquid to sustain their calorie needs that even tiny amounts of chemicals can become concentrated in their bodies. Worse, dyes form a coating on the surface of hummingbirds' tongues, reducing their effectiveness in drinking. Because hummingbirds quickly identify appropriate sources of food and remember the locations, it is unnecessary to use red dye to attract or maintain their habits. Honey is also mistakenly used as a source of sweetness in feeders, but this ingredient can also cause more harm than good because it often ferments and can foster the growth of dangerous bacteria, killing hummingbirds that ingest it. The only safe food for hummingbirds is white sugar and water. There are also commercial hummingbird nectar products, but these can be tricky to use, as some of the ingredients added to these mixes decompose quickly in sunlight and require constant monitoring to prevent spoilage.

Ants, bees, wasps, other birds, and bats are also attracted to hummingbird feeders. All of these visitors can be discouraged by using feeder models with insect guards. Feeders with yellow attractors may also be part of the problem, at least with bees and wasps, because these insects can detect the color yellow, but not red.

Perches on hummingbird feeders are not necessary, but are an advantage for the birds, as they reduce the energy used by hummingbirds when they are feeding.

Hummingbirds arrive and depart on their annual migrations at different times in different geographical locations. Local birding clubs and nature groups may be used to determine when feeders should first be hung in the spring and taken down in the fall. In general, hummingbirds can be expected from April through October in most of the country. The greatest activity, however, might not be experienced at the beginning of the season, when females are nesting and caring for young. When the new generation of hummingbirds leaves the nest, however — usually from June through July — an increase in numbers and activity may be noted at feeders until the birds head south for the winter.

RESOURCES

Organizations that deal with bird, animal, and wildlife issues can provide additional information about hummingbirds, as well as being useful in local, regional, or national efforts to protect natural habitats and endangered species.

NORTH AMERICAN WILD BIRD INFORMATION

American Birding Association
P.O. Box 6599
Colorado Springs, CO 80934
800-634-7736

The Hummer/Bird Study Group
P.O. Box 250, Clay, AL 35048

National Audubon Society
700 Broadway, New York, NY 10003
212-979-3100

The Nature Conservancy
1815 N. Lynn Street
Arlington, VA 22209
703-841-5300

Wild Bird Magazine
3 Burroughs, Irvine, CA 92718
714-8558822

HUMMINGBIRD FEEDERS AND SUPPLIES

Aspects, Inc.
245 Child Street, Warren, RI 02885

Burd Products
Box 580, Cedaredge, CO 81413
800-367-1245

Droll Yankee Inc.
27 Mill Road, Foster, RI 02825
1-800-352-9164

Hummingbird Haven
1255 Carmel Drive
Simi Valley, CA 93065

Hyde Bird Feeder Company
Box 168, Waltham, MA 02254

Perky-Pet Products
2201 S. Wabash Street
Denver, CO 80231

Rubbermaid, Inc.
1147 Akron Rd., Wooster, OH 44691

Wild Bird Centers of America, Inc.
7687 MacArthur Blvd.
Cabin John, MD 20818
1-800-WILDBIRD

Wild Birds Unlimited
11711 N. College Avenue, Suite 146
Carmel, IN 46032
1-800-326-4928

ONLINE RESOURCES

Computer connections to information can prove useful to those interested in wildlife and nature. Online resources include reference material, discussions with like-minded individuals, communications with agencies and organizations involved with wildlife, and access to up-to-date information and schedules. As the online industry is growing and evolving rapidly, listed resources may change and new resources may pop up unexpectedly. To search for additional resources, look for menu listings or search for topics associated with **birds**, **wildlife**, **wild animals**, **nature**, **ecology**, and **environmental resources**. Also look for topics listed by the common name of an animal, such as **hummingbird**.

Many libraries now provide access to their materials through online connections. Using terminals inside libraries — or dialing in from a remote location — use the same search strategies to locate books, reference material, and periodicals.

AMERICA ONLINE

Go to <Nature Conservancy> or <Birding>

COMPUSERVE

Go to <Earth Forum> or <Outdoor Network>

WORLD WIDE WEB

Hummingbirds   <http://www.derived.com/~lanny/hummers>

Birding on the Web   <http://www.birder.com>

Peterson online   <http://www.petersononline.com/birds>

Cornell Laboratory of Ornithology
        <http://www.ornith.cornell.edu/birdlab.html>

Smithsonian Migratory Bird Center
        <http://www.si.edu/natzoo/zooview/smbc/smbchome.htm>

BIBLIOGRAPHY

Allen, Elsa Guerdrum. *Transactions of the American Philosophical Society: The History of American Ornithology Before Audubon.* 1951, The American Philosophical Society (Philadelphia, PA).

Allen, Francis H., ed. *Thoreau on Birds: Notes on New England Birds from the Journals of Henry David Thoreau.* 1993, Beacon Press (Boston, MA). Originally published as Thoreau's Bird-lore, 1910, Houghton Mifflin.

American Ornithologists' Union. *Check-List of North American Birds.* 1957, American Ornithologists' Union.

Baird, S.F.; Brewer, T.M.; and Ridgway, R. *A History of North American Birds, Volume II, Land Birds.* 1874, Little, Brown, and Company.

Bent, Arthur Cleveland. *Life Histories of North American Cuckoos, Goatsuckers, Hummingbirds, and Their Allies.* 1940, Smithsonian Institution. Republished 1989, Dover Publications (Mineola, NY).

Benyus, Janine M. *The Field Guide to Wildlife Habitats of the Western United States.* 1989, Fireside/Simon & Schuster.

Boone, Elizabeth H. Transactions of the American Philosophical Society: *Incarnations of the Aztec Supernatural: The Image of Huitzilopochtli in Mexico and Europe.* 1989, The American Philosophical Society (Philadelphia, PA).

Bradfield, Maitland. *Birds of the Hopi Region, Their Hopi Names, and Notes on Their Ecology.* 1974, Northern Arizona Society of Science and Art, Inc. (Flagstaff, AZ).

Burton, Robert. *Bird Flight: An Illustrated Study of Birds' Aerial Mastery.* 1990, Facts on File (New York, NY).

Chapman, Frank M. *Handbook of Birds of Eastern North America.* 1932, D. Appleton & Company (New York, NY).

Choate, Ernest A. *The Dictionary of American Bird Names.* 1985, Harvard Common Press (Boston, MA).

Cleave, Andrew. *Hummingbirds.* 1990, Dorset Press (New York, NY).

Comstock, Anna Botsford. *Handbook of Nature Study.* 1911. Comstock Publishing Company Inc. Republished 1967, Cornell University Press (Ithaca, NY).

Coues, Elliott. *Key to North American Birds.* 1872, Dodd & Mead (New York, NY).

Cutright, Paul Russell. *The Great Naturalists Explore South America.* 1940, Books for Libraries Press/Macmillan Company.

Donnan, Christopher B. *Moche Art and Iconography.* 1976, UCLA Latin American Center Publications (Los Angeles, CA).

Doughty, Robin W. *Feather Fashions and Bird Preservation: A Study in Nature Protection.* 1975, University of California Press (Berkeley, CA).

Ehrlich, Paul R.; Dobkin, David S.; Wheye, Darryl. *The Birder's Handbook: A Field Guide to the Natural History of North American Birds.* 1988, Fireside/Simon & Schuster.

Feduccia, Alan, ed. *Catesby's Birds of Colonial America*. 1985, University of North Carolina Press (Chapel Hill, NC). Originally published as Natural History of Carolina, Florida, and the Bahama Islands, Mark Catesby, 1731–43.

Goodrich, S.G., and Winchell, Alexander. *Johnson's Natural History, Comprehensive, Scientific, and Popular, Illustrating and Describing the Animal Kingdom, with its Wonders and Curiosities*. 1867, A.J. Johnson & Company (New York, NY).

Grant, Karen A., and Grant Verne. *Hummingbirds and Their Flowers*. 1968, Columbia University Press (New York, NY).

Gray, Annie P. Bird Hybrids: *A Check-List with Bibliography*. 1958, Commonwealth Agricultural Bureaux (Bucks, England).

Greenewalt, Crawford H. *Hummingbirds*. 1990, Dover Publications Inc./first published 1960, American Museum of Natural History/Doubleday & Company.

Harrison, Colin. *A Field Guide to the Nests, Eggs and Nestlings of North American Birds*. 1978, Collins (New York, NY).

Headstrom, Richard. *Birds' Nests of the West: A Field Guide*. 1951, Ives Washburn, Inc. (New York, NY).

Howell, Steve N. G., and Webb, Sophie. *A Guide to the Birds of Mexico and Northern Central America*. 1995, Oxford University Press (New York, NY).

Hunt, Eva. *The Transformation of the Hummingbird: Cultural Roots of a Zinacantecan Mythical Poem*. 1977, Cornell University Press (Ithaca, NY).

Johnsgard, Paul A. *The Hummingbirds of North America*. 1983, Smithsonian Institution Press.

Kaufman, Kenn. Peterson Field Guide Series: *A Field Guide to Advanced Birding, Birding Challenges and How to Approach Them*. 1990, Houghton Mifflin Company.

Lazaroff, David Wentworth. *The Secret Lives of Hummingbirds*. 1995, Arizona-Sonora Desert Museum (Tucson, AZ).

Leahy, Christopher. *The Birdwatcher's Companion: An Encyclopedic Handbook of North American Birdlife*. 1982, Hill and Wang/Farrar, Straus and Giroux.

Lyon, Thomas J., ed. *This Incomparable Lande: A Book of American Nature Writing*. 1989, Houghton Mifflin.

Martin, Laura C. *The Folklore of Birds*. 1993, Globe Pequot Press (Old Saybrook, CT).

McGowan, Chris. *Diatoms to Dinosaurs: The Size and Scale of Living Things*. 1994, Shearwater Books/Island Press (Washington, DC).

Mearns, Barbara, and Mearns, Richard. *Audubon to Xántus: the Lives of Those Commemorated in North American Bird Names*. 1992, Academic Press/Harcourt Brace Jovanovich (San Diego, CA).

National Geographic Society. *Field Guide to the Birds of North America* (2nd edition). 1987, National Geographic Society (Washington, DC).

Newfield, Nancy L., and Nielsen, Barbara. *Hummingbird Gardens: Attracting Nature's Jewels to Your Backyard*. 1996, Chapters Publishing Ltd. (Shelburne, VT).

Parsons, Elsie Clews. *Pueblo Indian Religion*. 1996, University of Nebraska Press (Lincoln, NE). Originally published in 1939 by the University of Chicago Press.

Peabody, Selim H. *Cecil's Books of Natural History*. 1881, American Book Exchange (New York, NY).

Peterson, Roger Tory. *Peterson Field Guides: Western Birds*. 1961, Houghton Mifflin.

Proctor, Michael; Yeo, Peter; Lack, Andrew. *The Natural History of Pollination*. 1996, Timber Press (Portland, OR).

Proctor, Noble S., and Lynch, Patrick. *Manual of Ornithology: Avian Structure & Function*. 1993, Yale University Press (New Haven, CT).

Roe, Peter G. *The Cosmic Zygote: Cosmology in the Amazon Basin*. 1982, Rutgers University Press (New Brunswick, NJ).

Ruppell, Georg. *Bird Flight*. 1977, Van Nostrand Reinhold Company. First published in German in 1975 by Kindler Verlag GmbH (Munich, Germany).

Skutch, Alexander F. *Birds Asleep*. 1989, University of Texas Press (Austin, TX).

Skutch, Alexander. *The Life of the Hummingbird*. 1973, Vineyard Books/Crown Publishers Inc.

Spence, Lewis. *The Myths of Mexico and Peru*. 1914, Harrap (London). Republished 1977, Longwood Press (Boston, MA).

Stokes, Donald and Stokes, Lillian. *The Hummingbird Book: The Complete Guide to Attracting, Identifying, and Enjoying Hummingbirds*. 1989, Little, Brown and Company.

Swanton, John R. *Myths and Tales of the Southeastern Indians*. 1929, Bureau of American Ethnography/Smithsonian Institution, Bulletin 88.

Tree, Isabella. *The Ruling Passion of John Gould: A Biography of the British Audubon*. 1991, Grove Weidenfeld.

True, Dan. *Hummingbirds of North America: Attracting, Feeding, and Photographing*. 1994, University of New Mexico Press (Albuquerque, NM).

Tyler, Hamilton A. *Pueblo Birds and Myths*. 1979, University of Oklahoma Press (Norman, OK).

Tyrrell, Ester Quesada, and Tyrrell, Robert A. *Hummingbirds of the Caribbean*. 1990, Crown Publishers.

Welker, Robert Henry. *Birds and Men: American Birds in Science, Art, Literature, and Conservation, 1800–1900*. 1955, Belknap Press/Harvard University Press.

Wilbert, Johannes, ed. *Folk Literature of the Gê Indians*. 1978, UCLA Latin American Center Publications (Los Angeles, CA).

Zusi, Richard L., and Bentz, Gregory Dean. *Myology of the Purple-throated Carib (Eulampis Jugularis) and Other Hummingbirds (Aves: Trochilidae)*. 1984, Smithsonian Institution Press.

INDEX